AF600760
Wolf's cave
Lost Forest
Bears' cave
Old oak tree
ttage
Beaver dam
Rabbit grove

Charlie, Are You Daydreaming Again?

Stefanie Heyden & Fabian Grolimund

Charlie, Are You Daydreaming Again?

Illustrations by Marcus Wilke

Library of Congress Cataloging in Publication information for the print version of this book is available via the Library of Congress Marc Database under the LC Control Number 2024931384

Library and Archives Canada Cataloguing in Publication

Title: Charlie, are you daydreaming again? / Stefanie Heyden & Fabian Grolimund; illustrations by Marcus Wilke.
Other titles: Lotte, träumst du schon wieder? English
Names: Heyden, Stefanie, author. | Grolimund, Fabian, author. | Wilke, Marcus, illustrator.
Description: Translation of: Lotte, träumst du schon wieder? | Includes bibliographical references. | Translated from the German.
Identifiers: Canadiana (print) 2024030263X | Canadiana (ebook) 20240302737 | ISBN 9780889376359 (hardcover) | ISBN 9781613346358 (EPUB) | ISBN 9781616766351 (PDF)
Subjects: LCGFT: Picture books. | LCGFT: Fiction.
Classification: LCC PZ7.1.H49 Cha 2024 | DDC j833/.92-dc23

Original title: *Lotte, träumst du schon wieder?* by Stefanie Rietzler and Fabian Grolimund © 2020 by Hogrefe AG.
Translated from the German by Steven J. Pitock

www.hogrefe.com

PUBLISHING OFFICES

USA:	Hogrefe Publishing Corporation, 44 Merrimac Street, Suite 207, Newburyport, MA 01950 Phone 978 255 3700; E-mail customersupport@hogrefe.com
EUROPE:	Hogrefe Publishing GmbH, Merkelstr. 3, 37085 Göttingen, Germany Phone +49 551 99950 0, Fax +49 551 99950 111; E-mail publishing@hogrefe.com

SALES & DISTRIBUTION

USA:	Hogrefe Publishing, Customer Services Department, 30 Amberwood Parkway, Ashland, OH 44805 Phone 800 228 3749, Fax 419 281 6883; E-mail customersupport@hogrefe.com
UK:	Hogrefe Publishing, c/o Marston Book Services Ltd., 160 Eastern Ave., Milton Park, Abingdon, OX14 4SB Phone +44 1235 465577, Fax +44 1235 465556; E-mail direct.orders@marston.co.uk
EUROPE:	Hogrefe Publishing, Merkelstr. 3, 37085 Göttingen, Germany Phone +49 551 99950 0, Fax +49 551 99950 111; E-mail publishing@hogrefe.com

OTHER OFFICES

CANADA:	Hogrefe Publishing, 82 Laird Drive, East York, Ontario, M4G 3V1
SWITZERLAND:	Hogrefe Publishing, Länggass-Strasse 76, 3012 Bern

Printed and bound in the Czech Republic

ISBN 978-0-88937-635-9 (print) • ISBN 978-1-61676-635-1 (PDF) • ISBN 978-1-61334-635-8 (EPUB)
https://doi.org/10.1027/00635-000

For all girls, big or little:

It's ok to dream, discover, and invent.

It's ok to ask questions, make decisions, and speak your mind.

It's ok to dance. On a big stage or barefoot in the mud.

It's ok to grow and learn and reach your goals.

It's ok to fail.

It's ok to ask for help.

You can be loud or quiet, brave or afraid, silly or smart, rooted like a tree or free as a bird.

You are unique and strong and wonderful.

Life is offering you its hand.

– Stefanie Heyden –

For my seven-year-old son Gabriel, who has accompanied this story from the beginning. He motivated us while writing: "Are you still stuck?" He gave us compliments: "You've done a great job with the handyman!" And he gave us some very good feedback that led to important revisions: "Well, this part is totally boring, all they do is talk. You definitely have to improve that!"

– Fabian Grolimund –

Contents

A Hectic Morning

"Charlie, hurry up! Wash your ears, brush your teeth, and then off to school with you!" calls Mama Rabbit from the kitchen.
Upstairs in the bathroom, a little bunny girl is leaning up against the sink, staring at the stream of water running out of the faucet. Funny how the stream splits in two when you stick a paw in it! "Glug!" "Splish!" How it gurgles and splashes. As Charlie stands there, she starts dreaming... of the sea!

Storm. Rain. A pirate ship on the high seas. Charlie clutches the helm with both paws and pulls it around using her full weight. "Hoist the jib!" she yells against the wind tugging hard at her leather cape. The sails of her ship, the* ***Anne Bonny******, billow. The mast creaks as it strains against the wind. Massive waves swell and crash on the ship's hull. The pirate ship is shooting through the water swift as an arrow.*

* Hoist the jib: raise the triangular foresail of a ship.

** Anne Bonny was one of the most famous female pirates of all time, and Charlie's pirate ship is named after her. Anne Bonny was born in Ireland in 1698. Women were not allowed on pirate ships at that time, so she disguised herself as a man at first. She later teamed up with another famous pirate named Mary Read. From then on, the two sailed across the Caribbean and were notorious and feared plunderers.

Giant raindrops lash the faces of Charlie and her crew, Muriel the Duck and Frida the Bear. Suddenly, a bright bolt of lightning cracks over the sea. Look there! A shadow!

"Enemy in sight! Enemy in sight!" screeches Muriel the Duck, who is up on the lookout. "Frida, to the canons!"
Suddenly, Charlie feels a hand grip her shoulder.

"Char-lotte! Aren't you finished yet? Hurry up! You're not paying attention again!" Mama Rabbit sighs and looks at her wristwatch. "And you've got carrot juice on your face again. Quick, wash that out of your fur and brush your teeth. Else we'll both be late!"
"What?" Charlie looks up at her mother with wide eyes.
"You've got to ... oh come on, just let *me* do it. Mama Rabbit slides the toothbrush into Charlie's mouth. "It's always the same, every morning!" she complains, brushing her daughter's teeth and wiping her face.
Charlie lets her ears droop. "Why can't today be Saturday?" she thinks. "Then I could play all day and finish reading my pirate book about Anne Bonny."
Suddenly Charlie feels drowsy and heavy.
"Did you put your school things in your backpack?"
Charlie winces. "Oh darn!" With her mouth still full of toothpaste foam, she shakes her head.
"How many times do I have to remind you to pack your backpack the night before school?" asks her mother as she dashes into Charlie's bedroom.

"I'm so tired of this hassle," she grumbles as she quickly gathers pencils from Charlie's desk, picks up folders from the floor, and throws everything into the backpack.
Lost in thought, Charlie looks up at her. Her mother groans. "Charlie, don't just stand there. Here, take your backpack and go! Or you'll be late for school again."

Charlie is just about to say goodbye to her mother when the egg timer in the kitchen goes off. Mama Rabbit looks at her watch again.

"The cake, oh no! Ok, relax. On with the decoration and then off to work!"

She gives Charlie a quick kiss on the forehead.

A clearing with an old oak tree lies 633 paces away from the rabbits' house. Its gnarled trunk juts crookedly out of the ground as if wanting to take a bow. And if you look closely, you can see a heart carved into the rough bark with the names Charlie, Frida, and Muriel.

Frida the Bear carved it on the tree last summer with her sharp, pink-painted claws.

This morning, Frida has found herself a comfortable spot on a big root. She leans her shaggy back against the old oak tree. Her friend Muriel is running in circles around her, fluttering her duck wings excitedly and quacking:

"We'll be late, we'll be late! Mrs. Lynx is going to get mad! We'll be late!"

"Now stop running around like that. You're making me nervous," Frida grumbles, adjusting her pink bow.

Slowly, she stands up on her hind legs and straightens herself so high that her head bumps a branch.

"It's all right. Charlie's coming now!" she says, dropping to all fours with such force that the soft forest floor vibrates.

"Sorry, sorry! Thanks for waiting," Charlie pants, holding her side.

"Well, you're here now," Frida says and starts moving. It's still a long way to school.

As on every school day, the three friends walk through the forest side by side. Charlie inhales the cool, damp morning air and feels her heartbeat slow down. It smells of earth, moss, and damp wood. The first rays of sunlight fall through the canopy of leaves.

"So many different colors!" Charlie thinks and lets her gaze wander over the leaves shimmering in a thousand shades of green.

Suddenly Charlie's hind leg gets caught on a root and she stumbles. She manages to steady herself on a tree trunk just in time to keep from lurching onto the ground. Her eyes fall on the forest floor. But ... what is THAT?

Charlie excitedly calls to her friends: "Look, what a strange paw print! It's huge."

Muriel has already run ahead and is nervously swaying from one webbed foot to the other.

"I'm sure it's Mr. Beaver's. Maybe he's cutting down a tree nearby. Let's keep moving, we're going to be late."

Frida sighs: "Muriel is right. I guess we'll have to look at the paw print on the way home."

Charlie forces herself to turn away and runs to catch up with her friends.

"That certainly wasn't Mr. Beaver! The print is much bigger. I've never seen one like it before."

"Yes, yes, we'll look later," Muriel chatters and waddles ahead.

Charlie shakes her head and walks silently beside Frida the Bear. They both love the silence of the forest, broken only by the babbling of the little brook and the call of a cuckoo.

And by Muriel shouting out to them: “Hey, which tree has hanging cones again? The spruce or the fir?”
“Huh, why?” asks Charlie, scrunching up her face.
“Well, because of the test. I’m sure Mrs. Lynx will ask that question!” says Muriel and waddles on ahead.
“What test?” says Charlie.
“The one about trees,” grumbles Frida the Bear.
“But that’s not until next week,” insists Charlie, furrowing her forehead even deeper.
“No, it’s today, it’s today!” exclaims Muriel, fluttering her duck wings up and down.
Charlie stops abruptly, her head heating up and her whole body tingling. She stares at her friends, “What?!”
Muriel shakes her head. “Did you forget to write it down again?”

The Test

Screeeech! Mrs. Lynx, the teacher, runs her claws down the blackboard and the classroom quiets down immediately. No one dares make another sound.

"Good morning! Get out your English folders. We're going over the homework."

A loud rustling spreads through the class as everyone starts rummaging through their backpacks. In no time, Muriel, Frida, and the rest of the class all have their folders open. Only Charlie doesn't.

"Where the heck is my homework? Oh no! Didn't Mama put it in here?"

With trembling paws, Charlie searches through her backpack, but she can't find her English folder. Her heart is pounding madly, blood rushing to her ears.

"If I've forgotten my homework again, I'll definitely get detention!" she thinks. And she promised her mother she would stop forgetting so much.

"Come on, Charlotte. We're always waiting for you," says Mrs. Lynx in an irritated voice.

"I've got it," Charlie blurts out, grabbing the math folder and building a little privacy screen with her pencil case. "Please, please don't notice," she begs Mrs. Lynx inwardly.

"Then you can give us your answer to question one now, Charlotte. What did you write down?"
Charlie freezes and feels her stomach contract. What to say? Then Muriel nudges her under the bench with her wing and turns her English folder in Charlie's direction. Charlie rests her forehead on her paw so that nobody can see her peeking at Muriel's notes.
"Um, the blackbird ... um ... is sitting on the branch. So ... um ... blackbird and branch are the nouns."
Mrs. Lynx raises an eyebrow and approaches Charlie with quick steps.
"Good answer!"
She clutches Charlie's notebook and casts a critical glance at the math problems.
"Just not your own, unfortunately. You forgot your homework again, didn't you? That means detention for you next Wednesday! And Muriel, this is the last time you let Charlotte look at your homework! Or you'll get detention too!"
Charlie feels the eyes of the whole class on her and struggles to hold back tears. She doesn't even notice that Mrs. Lynx has started calling on the other children.
"I'm so stupid! Why does this always happen to me? I did my homework! Now I won't be able to play after school on Wednesday. Again! Mama will be so mad when she finds out!" she thinks.
The lesson goes on, but Charlie doesn't pay any attention.

During the test on trees, Mrs. Lynx keeps a close eye on her. Copying from Muriel or Frida is impossible. Charlie tries hard to remember the lessons.

"So, question three. Fir or spruce? Which tree is shown here?" she reads quietly and looks at the picture.

"Oh no, that's exactly what Muriel wanted to know this morning," Charlie remembers. "I have no idea ... I'll write fir. Fingers crossed ... Differences? With firs, the cones hang down, and with spruces, they stand up? What else could I write? Uh ... fir trees are bigger and they're used as Christmas trees."

Just as Charlie is about to start on the fourth question, Mrs. Lynx claps her paws three times.

"Pencils down, time's up. Charlotte, that goes for you too."

"I still have to write down my name," she stammers.

But Mrs. Lynx has already taken the test up from under her trembling paws.

After the school bell rings, Charlie takes a deep breath and loosens her shoulders. The weekend at last! Muriel, Frida, and Charlie pack up their school supplies and head home.

“Are you free to get together tomorrow?” asks Charlie.

“Yes, why don’t you come over to my house to play?” says Frida. “Papa is baking honey cake.”

“Great, I love his honey cake!” quacks Muriel.

While her friends discuss whether they should play boules, build a lean-to, or stay in the bears’ cave, Charlie examines the forest floor intently. “The paw print was here somewhere ... Ah yes, by that root over there! Strange, it’s gone ...” she thinks.

Just as she is about to tell her friends, Muriel’s chattering jolts her out of her thoughts: ” ... fortunately the test wasn’t that difficult ... except for that question about spruce and fir. I told you that would be on the test. What was your answer?”

“Could you please not talk about that stupid test? It’s the weekend,” Charlie moans, rolling her eyes.

“Alright, but first I want to know. I had to guess and I wrote down spruce.”

“Spruce is right,” says Frida.

Papa Rabbit Needs Charlie's Help

"Hi, Papa," Charlie calls out, popping her head through the open workshop door.

"Just a minute, sweetie. I need to outline the markings," answers Papa Rabbit without looking up from his workbench. With quick strokes, he draws on the wood in front of him.

"Done," he says, putting the pencil down and smiling at Charlie.

"What's this going to be?" asks Charlie. Papa Rabbit tells her about the Deer family who recently moved into the forest. During the move, a chest of drawers, a valuable family heirloom, got dropped. One drawer was broken, and the paint was chipped in several places.

"I'm trying to fix it," explains Papa Rabbit. "But for now, let's eat."

"What's for dinner?"

"Uh oh!" exclaims Papa Rabbit, slapping his paw over his mouth. "I forgot to go shopping!"

"Oh, Papa!" Charlie's stomach growls.

"We'll find something in the kitchen," says Papa. He lifts his daughter up with his strong arms, gives her a quick hug, and carries her through the workshop door.

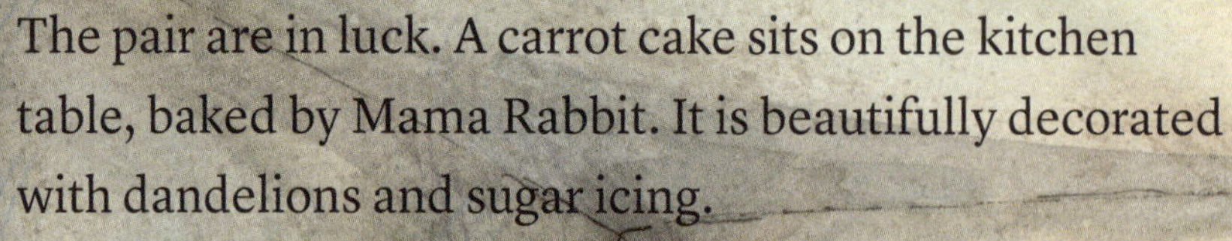

The pair are in luck. A carrot cake sits on the kitchen table, baked by Mama Rabbit. It is beautifully decorated with dandelions and sugar icing.

"Yum! Will you make some hot cocoa to go with it, Papa?" asks Charlie.

"Yes I will. And will you help me with the dresser later? The pattern on the top drawer is peeling off, so you'll have to trace it. You can do that better than me."

Charlie beams and nods eagerly. The two spend the entire afternoon in the workshop. Her father saws, planes, and sands while Charlie transfers the intricate floral pattern to the new drawer with fine, precise brush strokes.

“Finished!” she calls and washes out the brush.

Papa Rabbit tilts his head and carefully examines her work. “Charlie, that’s perfect. Mrs. Deer will be so pleased.”

Charlie leans against her father. The two look proudly at their joint work.

“Mama will be amazed when she comes home,”

Charlie thinks and feels a pleasant tingling in her body.

The evening sun falls through the workshop windows and the sawdust dances in the light. Suddenly the door is thrown open.

“There you are!” Mama Rabbit marches into the workshop. “You two ate the cake! What in the world were you thinking?”

Charlie and her father turn around.

“There was this order from the Deer family and I ...” Papa Rabbit starts to explain.

Mama Rabbit, breathing rapidly, starts to rant: “You know very well that we have visitors today.

It’s *your* turn to shop on Fridays. How many times do I have to remind you?”

“Dear, we only ate two slices. There’s a whole lot left.”

“You mean you want me to serve a cake that’s been cut into already? That would be embarrassing. I went to all that trouble, and now the decoration is ruined!”

“It’s only your brother coming over for dinner. He doesn’t care if we’ve already eaten a piece ...”

“The cake was meant for our guest. Period! And you knew that!” Mama Rabbit glares at him.

Charlie can’t take any more shouting. “Do you always have to be so loud when you’re mad, Mama?” she complains.

“It’s just too much! I always have to do everything! I work for hours, and then, when I finally get home, the cake I got up extra early to bake is half gone! And on top of that Mrs. Lynx called. Charlie, we worked on that English homework for two hours yesterday, and you left it at home!”

“I’m sorry,” Charlie mutters, her shoulders drooping.

“If you would just pack your backpack at night, you wouldn’t get detention,” her mother says.

“Let it go, sweetheart,” interrupts Papa Rabbit, “detention is punishment enough.”

Mama Rabbit puts both paws to her forehead as if she has a headache.

“It wears me out!

Mrs. Lynx said that Charlie hardly wrote anything in the test about trees. She forgot to tell me they were taking a test – again! It can't be that hard to keep a homework calendar."

Charlie defends herself, "I did write it down, I just put it in the wrong week! Besides, Rowena didn't have her homework yesterday either, and she didn't get detention! Mrs. Lynx is so unfair. She just doesn't like me."

"Enough of your excuses," groans Mama Rabbit. "Surely I can expect a third grader to keep track of her tests and homework!"

Charlie has a lump in her throat and tears well up in her eyes. Mama just doesn't get it!

"You're so mean!" she screams, running into the house and locking herself in her room with shaking paws. She throws herself on the bed, buries her hot face in the pillow, and soaks the pillow with her tears.

A little later, the front doorbell rings: "Ding dong!"

Muffled by the pillow feathers and the bedroom door, Charlie hears her father call out, "Charlie, Uncle Louis is here!"

With a jerk, she turns over and pulls the blanket over her head.

Uncle Louis' Good Idea

It's already dark outside when Charlie is woken up by a knock on her bedroom door.

"Charlie? I have to leave soon, but I'd still like to see you. Will you let me in?" she hears Uncle Louis say from the other side of the door. Charlie rubs her eyes, shuffles across her room, and turns the key.

"Ahoy pirate, who's hanging the jib?"* asks Uncle Louis, a bag in one hand and a plate of carrot cake in the other. "You missed the booty! But I brought you some."

"Thanks, landlubber!"**

With a grin, Charlie takes the cake and sits on the edge of her bed. Uncle Louis pulls off the camera hanging around his neck by a leather strap and places it on Charlie's desk. He sits down cross-legged on the floor.

"Have you all been arguing?"

Charlie shoves a piece of cake into her mouth and nods.

"Your mother told me about it. I think she was very sorry for what she said to you."

"But she's always like that," Charlie says. "She's always stressing me out and criticizing: 'Hurry up!

* Hanging the jib: pirate slang for pouting or frowning.

** Landlubber: derogatory word for a person who is not used to going to sea.

You're so forgetful! Pay attention! It's going to get bad if you don't stop!' Blah blah blah!"

"Your mother just worries a lot. But yeah, I'd lock myself in my room too. I know how you feel, it used to be the same with me."

And then Uncle Louis starts to tell Charlie about her grandparents, who constantly worried about his bad grades and his forgetfulness, always wondering what would become of him. Charlie can't believe it because Uncle Louis is such a successful photographer now.

"It used to be really bad," says Uncle Louis. "Do you want to hear an embarrassing story? I loved taking pictures even when I was in high school. One of my teachers thought I was good and asked me to take pictures on graduation day. I was so proud and wanted to take the best graduation pictures ever."

"What happened?"

"I photographed the whole thing. Shot all the great moments. But when I went to develop the photos, I realized I had forgotten to put a film in the camera. There wasn't a single photo of the graduation. Everyone was so disappointed! All my classmates and their parents. That was a really big mess ..."

Charlie's eyes widen and she pats Uncle Louis' arm – she knows exactly how it feels to disappoint people.
"But now this doesn't happen to you anymore?" she wants to know.
Uncle Louis grins. "I have a trick. At the right moment, I tell myself what I have to do. That works for homework and tests too, by the way."
Charlie is excited to hear that. She wants to know more about Uncle Louis' trick. Together they design a poster:

My "When-Then Plan"

To make sure I don't forget anything important, I tell myself what I must remember to do in certain situations.

When Mrs. Lynx writes a homework assignment on the board, then I take out my homework notebook and write it down right away.

When I finish a homework assignment, then I put it in my backpack right away.

When Mrs. Lynx announces a test, then I take out my homework notebook right away, flip to the correct date, write it down, and highlight it.

Uncle Louis suggests that Charlie take a little imaginary journey to practice the plan.

"So, Charlie, if you want, you can close your eyes. Imagine you're in your classroom, Muriel is sitting next to you. Maybe you see Frida, too – look around a bit. Who's there? Mrs. Lynx is standing at the front of the classroom. Now she turns to the blackboard and says, 'For your homework, you will … .' and then she writes the assignment on the blackboard. What do you say to yourself?"

"When Mrs. Lynx writes a homework assignment on the board, then I take out my homework notebook and write it down right away!"

"Great. You copy everything written on the blackboard and check again to make sure it's all written down! Maybe you're even a little proud of yourself because you remembered your plan?"

Charlie lies there, eyes closed. "It's like going to the movies, but this movie is boring!"

"A movie with you in the leading role can never be boring!" replies Uncle Louis, laughing. "Come on, let's rewind and watch your inner movie a few more times!"

The second and third time, Charlie can imagine the situation much more clearly. The sentence she memorized comes to mind as soon as Mrs. Lynx writes "homework" on the board.

Uncle Louis has another trick up his sleeve.

Homework

He goes to get his instant camera out of the car and asks Charlie to go to her desk and playact doing homework. "Show me what you look like copying homework off the board." Click! "Now take a worksheet and pretend it's homework you're putting in your backpack." Click! The instant camera spits out the pictures and Louis writes Charlie's when-then sentences on the pictures in beautiful, squiggly writing.

"There, you can put those in your pencil case to help you remember."

At that moment, Mama Rabbit pokes her head into the room: "Hey, you two, it's almost bedtime. And, Louis, you should be getting home."

"We'll be ready in a minute," Uncle Louis says, winking at Charlie. He reaches into his bag and pulls out a mysteriously shaped package.

"What's this?" asks Charlie, eyeing the object covered in newspaper and tape.

"Open it!"

Charlie carefully loosens the strips of tape and pulls the layers of newspaper apart.

"A pirate ship!

And it even says *Anne Bonny* on the hull!" she exclaims with shining eyes. "Where did you get that?"

Uncle Louis smiles. "Last week I photographed a small fishing village for a magazine. I found a tiny store there, in an old lighthouse. You would have loved it: full of shells, sea urchin skeletons, old oil lamps, shark teeth. And when I saw that ship, it made me think of you. So I got the owner of the store, an old walrus, to inscribe 'Anne Bonny' on it for you."

"Thanks, Uncle Louis!"

Charlie very carefully puts the new caravel* on her nightstand so that she can look at it as she falls asleep. She hugs her uncle.

"There, now off to your berth** – and I have to get going."

Uncle Louis gets up, kisses Charlie on the forehead, and heads for the door.

"Uncle Louis?" says Charlie.

"Yes?"

"Your camera!"

"I've got it right here," he says, holding up the instant camera.

"Not that one. The other one!"

"Oh thank you! I completely forgot that."

* Caravel: a sailing ship with two to four masts.

** Berth: a shelf-like sleeping space on a ship.

After Uncle Louis has left, Mama Rabbit slips into the room. Quickly, Charlie closes her eyes and pretends to be fast asleep. She feels the mattress flatten a bit when Mama Rabbit sits down, and soon she feels a gentle caress on her head.

Barely audibly, her mother whispers: "Oh, bunny, I'm sorry. All I want is for you to do well."

The Wolf's Howl

In the middle of the night, Charlie bolts up in bed, "What was that?"

Anxiously, she casts her gaze about her moonlit room. There it is again: a long-drawn-out "Ahhwooooo!"

Charlie's fur stands on end, a shiver creeping down her spine. She shrieks, grabs her stuffie, and dashes out of her room into the dark hallway. Fortunately, when she shoves open the door to the master bedroom, her father is already awake and sitting up in bed.

"Did you have a bad dream?"

"Di-di-didn't you hear it?" stammers Charlie. "Out there? That ... ahhwooooo! There it is again!"

"Oh, that." Papa Rabbit puts a paw on her shoulder reassuringly. "That's a wolf's howl."

"What? Wolves! In our woods?"

"Yes, one has been prowling the Lost Forest for a long time. It's rare to hear its howl all the way over here at our place. They say the wolf lives in the old cave. No one knows for sure – no one has been to that part of the forest for years. And you're not allowed to go there either, you know that."

"Because of the wolf?"

"Because it's dangerous. Mr. Beaver, the forest ranger, says that there are rotten trees in the Lost Forest that can fall at any time. Besides, the trees are so close together and so overgrown that hardly any light gets through – it's gloomy even during the day and it's easy to get lost in there."
"And the wolf?"
"No one has seen him yet. He keeps to his territory. Now go back to bed."
Charlie would have loved to crawl into bed with her parents, but Papa Rabbit thinks she's too old for that.

The way back along the dark hallway seems endless to her. "Why is the wolf howling like that? What if he does come here? Maybe that huge paw print on the path to school is his! What do I do if he sneaks in through the window?"

She sits down on the edge of her bed. "I need light. I'll light a candle!"

Charlie's parents had forbidden this – it's dangerous to leave candles burning at night – but tonight there's no way round it. The wooden match breaks. She struck it too hard! Again. Finally, the candle burns, the light flickers, and shadows dance around the room. Charlie rummages through her pirate chest, pulls out the wooden cutlass, and crawls under her blanket with it. "If he jumps in through the window, I'll whack him with the cutlass," she tells herself.

Best Friends

The next day, Charlie sets off for the Bear family's den. When she gets there, she reaches for the heavy iron ring on the door, knocks three times, and Papa Bear opens the door to greet her. "Come in," he says. "The others are in Frida's room." Charlie offers her paw to Papa Bear, which he envelopes in two enormous, furry paws. "It smells so yummy in here," she gushes, sniffing the air. Papa Bear grins. "Honey cake with a pudding center. But it's just come out of the oven and needs a little longer to cool. I'll call you when it's ready."

Charlie hears loud laughter coming from Frida's room. When she goes in, she discovers her friends sitting on the bed looking at a magazine.

Mon Tu We Th Fr

"What are you doing?" Charlie wants to know.

"Some silly test in the new Sparkle magazine," Muriel quacks and giggles. "Do you want to know what friendship type Frida is?"

Charlie hops onto Frida's bed in one big leap and sits down right next to her friend on the soft blanket. Muriel flips the page with a flap of her wings and puts on a serious expression.

"Now for the results. Frida, you're friendship type B: the loyal soul."

Charlie smiles and leans against Frida's soft fur. "Who would have thought that?"

"Quiet now, I'm reading the rest. Alright. The loyal soul. Your friends can always count on you. People bring their problems to you. You are great at listening. You never make fun of anyone and are always honest. But make sure you don't sell yourself short. You have the coziest room of all – the best place to hang out with your friends."

Frida grins. "I'm sure it doesn't say that about the room. Let me see," she says, snatching the magazine from Muriel's wing.

"That's a good one!" Charlie giggles.

Muriel looks around the room. "Say, Frida, what did you do with all those ballet photos?"

"Took 'em down," Frida grumbles.

Just then they hear a call from the kitchen. The cake is ready! Charlie sniffs the air again. How wonderful, the smell of cinnamon and honey! Frida says they should eat the cake in her room and sets off to get three pieces.

As Frida shuts the door behind her, Charlie asks: " Any idea why she took down the photos?"

"No," Muriel replies. "Just because she doesn't go to ballet anymore doesn't mean she has to take them down, does it?"

Muriel flutters to the other corner of the room and picks up one of the photos that had been taken down. "She looks great!"

Just at that moment, Frida enters the room with the cake platter. "Put that down right now!" she growls.

Instantly, Muriel puts the picture back onto the pile and flutters back onto the bed.

Charlie winces a little, surprised. "Hey Frida, what's the matter? Did we do something wrong?"

She looks at her friend questioningly. "I don't understand why you don't go to ballet anymore. You always loved it, didn't you?"

Frida turns away silently and stares at the floor.

"You can tell us. We're your friends, your best friends!" says Muriel, stroking Frida's back with her wing.

"Is it because of the new teacher? That Mrs. Peacock?" Charlie reaches out her paw too.

Frida drops her head to her chest, her eyes filling with tears. "She said it looks ridiculous when a fat bear dances on stage with everyone."

"What nonsense! It's not true at all! You look so elegant when you dance!" Charlie is upset.

And Muriel quacks, "What an outrageous thing to say! She can't really have said that.

"Yeah, but, she did!" sobs Frida. "Mrs. Peacock wants to put on a ballet, *Swan Lake*, and she only wants the elegant swans in it. She told me I could dance in the very back during rehearsals, but not during the performance."

Muriel and Charlie try to comfort their friend. They tell her how admirably she danced at the last rehearsal and how talented she is.

But when Muriel says, "And you're not fat at all. You're just strong. Bears ... simply are stout ...," Frida only starts sobbing even louder and doesn't want to eat any more of her favorite cake.

Suddenly Muriel grins broadly. "I've got something that will cheer you up!" she quacks, picking up her backpack. She reaches inside and pulls out three friendship bracelets.

"Look, I made these for us, I made them myself!" explains Muriel excitedly. "Do you like them?"

She stretches out her wing and shows her friends three bracelets knitted out of yarn.

"What do you think, do you like them? I picked out our three favorite colors: pink for Frida, purple for Charlie, and blue for me!"

Charlie reverently takes her bracelet and slips it over her paw.

She beams at Muriel, who puts her bracelet around her neck like a necklace.

Frida grumbles, "Bit tight," tugging hard, trying to get the ribbon over her paw.

"Watch out, watch out, you're going to break it, it's going to break!" Muriel quacks, waddling excitedly around Frida.

Charlie has an idea: "You know what would look good? If you put the bracelet on your ear. Lean down over here, I'll help you."

Frida bends down to Charlie as she stands on tiptoe and slips the bracelet over her friend's left ear. It fits perfectly.

"All we need now is an oath of friendship," Charlie suggests.

The three exchange ideas briefly, then stand in a circle and take each other by the paws and wings.

"We swear to remain best friends forever and let nothing and no one tear us apart. A promise is solemn, never to be broken."

The afternoon flies by. The girls play their favorite record on the old record player that Frida inherited from her grandpa, singing along at the top of their voices, and dancing around the room. Everything – Mrs. Peacock, school, the trouble Charlie had with her parents – is forgotten for the moment.

"Frida!" calls Papa Bear from the kitchen eventually. "Your mother will be here soon. We'll eat in half an hour!"

"Should I ask if you can stay for dinner?" Frida wants to know.

Muriel agrees enthusiastically because Mr. and Mrs. Bear run the "Bear's Paw" bakery and pastry shop, and for dinner Frida's mother always brings the leftovers: cinnamon buns, honey rolls, croissants, Danishes, cakes, and fresh bread.

Charlie hesitates. "It will be dark by the time we've finished dinner. I think I'd better go home now."

Frida and Muriel stare at her in disbelief. "But why? Since when are you afraid of the dark?"

Charlie tries to explain, "Did you know that there is a wolf in the Lost Forest? I heard him howling last night. It was scary!"

"A wolf! I've never seen a wolf there," says Muriel.

"Neither have I," says Frida. "But we hear its howl a lot. Papa thinks the wolf comes from the north. There, they still follow the old ways."

"The old ways?" Muriel wants to know. She looks a little uneasy.

"Well, you know. Like in the olden days," Frida murmurs.

"What do you mean?" asks Charlie.

Frida gulps and mutters: "In the north, wolves still hunt."

Charlie can't believe her ears. Does that really still happen?! She feels hot and cold all at once, and her fur stands on end. Muriel flutters around the room so wildly that she loses a few feathers, and quacks, "They hunt, they hunt! The wolf will eat us!"

Frida tries to calm her friends. “Hold on. He hasn’t eaten anyone yet. And Papa says he’s been living in the Lost Forest for a while and will stay there.”

But Muriel wants to go home right away, too. Charlie is glad that she and Muriel can walk together until they get to the crossroads at the old oak tree. Then they both run the rest of their separate ways home as fast as their legs can carry them.

I Hate Homework!

Sunday. What a beautiful day! After breakfast, Charlie grabs her sketch pad and charcoal pencil and hops happily outside. There, a stag beetle! The magnificent insect crawls slowly across an old tree trunk. Charlie sits very still and observes it closely: the enormous mandibles that look like antlers, the dark brown carapace with a slight reddish glow, and the finely serrated legs. Charlie carefully takes her charcoal pencil in her paw and begins to draw.

A few minutes later, Mama Rabbit hops up behind her, “Here you are, I’ve been looking everywhere for you!”

Charlie looks up from her drawing and proudly holds out the pad to her mother. “Look, a stag beetle!”

Mama Rabbit glances at it and says, “It’s a good drawing.”

Charlie smiles and continues drawing. But Mama Rabbit squints at her watch and takes a deep breath. “You know, we agreed that you would practice next week’s dictation after breakfast.”

Charlie sighs, “But I haven’t finished my drawing yet.”

“You can finish later. Come along now, please, I don’t have all day. I have to do the laundry and make lunch.”
Charlie doesn’t move.

Mama Rabbit tilts her head and taps her wristwatch.
"I'm waiting!"
"The beetle will be gone later," Charlie mutters and folds the sketch pad shut. Slowly, she plods into the house behind her mother.
A little later, the two are sitting at the dining table. To Charlie, the dictation feels endless. She can hardly concentrate at all. Soon her head feels hot and heavy. When she tries to rest her chin on her paw, Mama Rabbit shakes her head.
"Come on! Pay attention, Charlie, only one more sentence! So: The leaves drift down the river."
Charlie looks out of the window. "I bet the stag beetle is already gone!" she thinks.
"Charlie, keep your eyes on your work!" Mama Rabbit rolls her eyes. "You could have finished by now. Write this down now: The leaves ... drift ... down ... the river."
Finally, the last sentence is finished. Charlie drops the pen and rubs her eyes. Her mother takes the page and begins to underline all the mistakes. Each time Mama Rabbit makes a mark with the red pen, Charlie winces inwardly. In the end, she writes "22 mistakes" at the bottom of the page.
"We practiced that! But you made exactly the same mistakes again!" sighs Mama Rabbit in an exasperated voice.
"Your mind is just not focused. Look at all these careless mistakes: You forgot to dot the i's, you wrote 'leafs' for 'leaves.' And the word 'river' should not be capitalized.

You know that! Only the names of specific rivers are capitalized. I'm afraid we'll have to write it again."

Charlie feels like she can't breathe anymore. It's all too much for her. Doesn't anyone notice how hard she's trying? How tired she is? Her eyes begin to burn. The page of dictation starts to blur as she looks at it, and slowly a tear rolls down her furry cheek.

"I can't do this! I'm just too stupid!" she sobs in despair, burying her face in her arms.

As she does, her pencil case sails off the table and a few pencils roll across the floor.

Mama Rabbit sighs, then lovingly strokes Charlie's head. "You're not stupid!" she says.

"I can't do all this!" cries Charlie, choking with tears.

Her mother pulls Charlie into her arms. "I don't like it either. But the dictation test is in three days and you don't want another bad grade, do you? I just want to help you," she says softly into Charlie's fur.

When Charlie finishes crying, her face is all puffy. She feels tired and empty.

Her mother stands up, picks up the pencil case and pencils from the floor, and says, "I think we'll have to postpone dictation until the evening."

Charlie is relieved. "Can I go to Muriel's? She's looking after her siblings today and she's probably bored," she asks her mother.

"Maybe later," Mama Rabbit replies. "Do your homework first. You still have some assignments to finish from your homework list for this week. And you know how Mrs. Lynx feels about unfinished homework."

"Can't I do it later?" begs Charlie. "It's so much, and I want to go to Muriel's for a bit first, please Mama."

But Mama Rabbit persists. "Business before pleasure! If you buckle down and get on with it, you'll have it all done in an hour and then you can go see Muriel."

Charlie sinks back into her chair. It's going to be a long day.

This Is Who I Am

Like every morning, Muriel and Frida are waiting for their friend Charlie at the old oak tree. And like almost every morning, Charlie arrives late, running.

Muriel frowns. “Next time, we’ll go without you! We have to write an essay first thing at school today. We never have enough time for those!” she complains and waddles on ahead.

“Sorry. Papa was supposed to wake me up today but he overslept,” Charlie pants.

Muriel lets out a loud breath. “Why didn’t you come by my house yesterday? You promised!”

Charlie immediately feels guilty. When Muriel’s mother has to work weekends at the café, Muriel is left alone with her eight little brothers and sisters and has to look after them, cook, and clean up. The last time Charlie cooked snail stew with Muriel, they let the little rascals out of their sight for just one second. The chicks went to play tag in the pond, then waddled back into the house with their dirty webbed feet and jumped onto chairs, tables, sofas, and beds. Muriel would probably have been glad of Charlie’s help yesterday!

"I'm sorry. Mama wouldn't let me go because I hadn't finished my stupid homework. It took forever, and after dinner I had to practice dictation again," Charlie says.

"Aha." Muriel folds her wings behind her back and marches on hurriedly.

"Bear taxi, anyone?" Frida changes the subject.

"Yes!" Muriel and Charlie shout in unison and climb joyfully onto Frida's back. The bear rambles off, carrying her friends to school with long, swift strides.

Soon, Charlie is staring up at the essay topic Mrs. Lynx has written on the blackboard: "This Is Who I Am. Describe yourself using as many adjectives as possible."

"This is who I am ... who I am ...," Charlie mumbles to herself, plucking at the bracelet Muriel gave her. "What in the world is everybody writing? I can't think of anything at all!"

Charlie looks around the classroom. She hears the scratching of pens on paper and sees that her classmates are filling up their pages.

Muriel writes so fast that Charlie even feels a slight breeze from her wings gliding quickly across the paper.

Charlie has written only a few sentences. She reads through what she has written so far:

"This is me. i am Charlie. i am ten years old. I am a bunny and live in rabbitgrove."

"Gosh, what else am I supposed to write?" she wonders.

Suddenly, Mrs. Lynx's shadow falls onto her page. "The others are almost done and you have barely started!" the teacher says through her teeth. "I want at least two pages from you! Don't be the only one who hands in an almost blank page again."

"Yes, Mrs. Lynx," Charlie stammers, lowering her eyes.

"And read the assignment carefully! You're supposed to use adjectives. Now concentrate!" admonishes Mrs. Lynx, tapping a claw on Charlie's sheet of paper.

"Adjectives ... adjectives," the word swirls in Charlie's mind. "Who am I?" Finally, she begins to write:

This Is Who I Am

i am Charlie. i am 10 years old. I am a bunny and live in rabbitgrove my favarit color is purpul and i my favarit food is carrot cake with dandylion pieces. i have two best friends They are called Frida and Muriel. i like to draw and make things.
Everyone says i am to slow. And that I do not lissen or pay attention and I do not consentrate. And that I for- that I am forgetful and that no one can rely on me.
althouh that is actuly unfair because ever since uncle Louis showed me his trick I always remember my home work!! But nobody noticed. my parents often get angry at me and are always complaining becase i cannot rite good and get bad grades. but I do not do that on purpose. i hate school.
i can't do anything well exsept drawing and that does not count. Mama is sometimes sad and says that if things keep going like this she is woried about my futur. And then I don't know what to say.
and i can't rite two pages.
and i don't know what stupid agjectives are and where to rite them.

"Pencils down! Time's up!" Mrs. Lynx calls as she starts to collect the essays.

Detention

Two days later, Wednesday afternoon, Charlie has to stay on after school for detention.
Mrs. Lynx lays a poem and a blank sheet of paper on her desk: "When you've finished copying the poem, you can go.
No more than two mistakes!"
Charlie skims the lines and starts counting the words: "393! It's so long!" she thinks.
With a deep sigh, she begins to write. After a long while, she shakes out her cramped-up paw. It really is a long poem! And so many difficult words that she doesn't even understand!
Mrs. Lynx, sitting at the teacher's desk correcting essays, gives her a stern look.
"Keep going, Charlotte, or you'll still be sitting here tomorrow."
Charlie lowers her eyes, grabs her pen and continues writing:

"... Fire!" was the awful shout,
as smoke from cabin* and hatch** poured out,
first smoke, then flames, a blazing glow ... "

* Cabin: room in a ship where you live and sleep.
** Hatch: opening on a ship that can be closed with a board on hinges.

"A blazing glow," Charlie thinks and absentmindedly chews on her pen. Her vision blurs, and she plunges into her dream world.

The pirate ship **Anne Bonny*** *is being tossed back and forth by the waves. Water splashes over the deck, which becomes so slippery that Charlie has to hold onto the ship's railing. Lightning flashes again. Charlie blinks in the light and then freezes: Directly in front of them a mighty pirate ship appears from the shadows, huge as a sea monster.*
*"It's the Nightmare!** cries Muriel.*
Charlie's heart skips a beat. "Frida! To the cannon!"
Charlie has to shout against the raging storm. Just then she hears the thunder of enemy guns and the splintering of wood. She turns around. A big hole has been shot through the railing. The heavy, pungent smell of gunpowder wafts into her nose.
Below deck, Frida brings the cannon into position. She holds the torch to the fuse. A loud boom! The **Anne Bonny** *trembles. A massive iron ball whizzes through the darkness and bores deep into the hull of the enemy Nightmare. Cannonballs fly back and forth between the two ships.*

* The **Anne Bonny** is Charlie's pirate ship, named after a famous female pirate.

** The Nightmare is a three-masted pirate ship captained by a female pirate named Savage Claw.

Again and again, cannons flare up and flash a ghostly light across the sea. And then: Charlie steers the ***Anne Bonny*** *to starboard* and Frida ignites the cannon at exactly the right moment.*
A mighty crash!
An enormous column of fire explodes through the hull of the enemy Nightmare. *Frida has hit a powder keg!***
"Board the ship!" Charlie shouts and brandishes her cutlass.

Charlie is startled by another sudden bang: "Charlotte! Are you daydreaming again?!"
In front of her, she sees the ruler Mrs. Lynx used to rap the desktop. Charlie shakes her head and needs a moment to remember where she is. In detention. At school. With Mrs. Lynx, who looks very annoyed.
"Where was I again ...?" stammers Charlie. Her gaze falls on the poem and the page in front of her. She has pressed her pen to the page with her paw all this time and created a big stain.
"Look at that mess!" says Mrs. Lynx, digging a claw into the ink stain.

'Fire!' was the awful shout,
as smoke from cabin and
hatch poured out,
first smoke, then flames,
a blazing glow

* Starboard: the right side of the ship as you're standing on it facing forward.
** Powder keg: a barrel of gunpowder.

"This is where you stopped. Barely halfway. Keep writing!" Charlie furtively glances at the clock. How much longer can detention last? Sentence by sentence, she struggles through the poem. If only she could write faster! Muriel would surely be finished by now. Impatiently, she slides back and forth on her chair. It's so uncomfortable!

She writes. And writes. Then Mrs. Lynx appears in front of her again.

"What now?" thinks Charlie.

Mrs. Lynx walks around Charlie's desk and stops next to her. From above, the teacher scrutinizes the paper. Charlie knows she has been too slow, and she is far from finished. After a moment's silence, the teacher gently puts her paw on Charlie's shoulder.

"That's enough," she says, "You've done enough work."

Did Charlie hear right? She gets to leave early?! Out of the corner of her eye, she sees that Mrs. Lynx is holding her essay in the other paw. Charlie breathes a sigh of relief and packs up her things. Finally!

As she walks through the forest on her way home, her mind wanders back to her pirate ship.

"Board the ship!" shouts Charlie, pointing her cutlass at the enemy ship.

"Aye, aye, Captain!" shouts Muriel, fluttering down from the lookout with pistols drawn.

Frida lumbers up the stairs and throws the heavy grappling hook over onto the enemy ship. With all her might, she pulls the **Anne Bonny** *toward the* Nightmare *until the ships' hulls touch. The three brave pirates jump over. An epic fight breaks out.*

Charlie bravely charges ahead with Muriel and Frida right behind her. Charlie's field of vision narrows, she feels her heart pumping faster, every muscle is tense. With a firm grip, she holds her cutlass in her paw: "Show yourself, Savage Claw!" she yells, ready for a fight.

Where is the lynx hiding?

The wind carries the sound of vicious laughter to her ears: "Ha ha ha! You dared board my ship? You hopped to your doom, you miserable rabbit!"

Charlie snorts and turns her head searchingly. Where did that voice come from? There! Her enemy is standing on the stern, legs wide apart. Savage Claw, the lynx, bares her teeth and hisses so fearsomely that Muriel takes cover behind Frida. Raindrops pelt the shoulders of Savage Claw's blood-red coat.*

"Seize these wretches!"

At that moment, three ghastly figures charge out of the darkness toward Charlie. They're the rabid triplets One Ear, One Eye, and Peg Leg. Badgers with foaming mouths, mangy fur, blood-shot eyes, and claws so sharp and long they cut grooves into the deck

* Stern: the rear of a ship.

with every step. One is missing an ear, one an eye, the third a leg – that's the only way to tell them apart. They give off a foul smell.

Next to Charlie, Frida pulls herself up to her full height: "Leave them to me – you take care of Savage Claw!" she growls.

The triplets advance, drawing their rusty swords, wheezing, snot dripping from their nostrils. Frida sounds a deafening roar. Briefly, the triplets freeze, their red eyes wide in shock. Peg Leg even loses his footing and slips on his brothers' snot and drool.

"Now," Frida roars and lunges at the triplets. While Frida swipes with her paw and hurls One Ear against the mast, Charlie runs past them up the stairs, her coat flapping in the wind.

In the meantime, Peg Leg has got back up again. Joining forces with his brother One Eye, he attacks Frida. The bear deftly dances away from their sword strokes, reaches out fast as lightning to One Eye, clamps him under one arm and clobbers his behind with two swift blows. She holds onto the other attacker by clamping her teeth around his wooden leg and then hurls him into the air in a high arc. He gets caught in a sail, whining and cursing. Eager to fight, Frida looks around, searching for more opponents.

Muriel stands behind Frida with pistols drawn and knees shaking. She can hardly move. Suddenly: a click!

Muriel wheels around, looks up at the mast, and spots a bundle of fur in the crow's nest. Muriel shields her eyes from the rain with a wing and peers through the darkness. There! It's moving! First a bushy tail appears and then a mighty crossbow slides up and over the edge of the crow's nest, pointing at Charlie! Without thinking, Muriel pulls the triggers. Both pistols flash. The bullets shred the crossbow and pieces of metal rain onto the deck. The crossbowman scurries down the mast with a shrill squeal. It's Tyra the Terrible, the squirrel with the long, rotten incisor. With her mouth wide open, she pounces on Muriel. But in mid air she is jerked back. Frida has caught her tail! Helplessly, Tyra dangles from Frida's paw. She tries to sink her rotten tooth into the bear's arm but lands in an empty water barrel instead. Frida slams the heavy lid shut. Tyra's raving and ranting can't help her now.

Muriel lowers her pistols and stammers, "That was close, way too close."

At the stern, the battle between Charlie and Savage Claw rages on. The two circle each other, out of breath. The lynx thrusts her long dagger. But Charlie counters with her cutlass and deflects the blow just in time. Metal screeches against metal. Then the lynx's extended claws rush toward Charlie's face.

She pulls her head back just in time to see the lynx's paw whizz right past her nose. Savage Claw is about to lunge again with her dagger when Charlie whacks the lynx's head with the handle of her cutlass. Silently, her enemy collapses, unconscious.

The rain continues to fall. The ship sways. Frida rushes over to Charlie and grabs Savage Claw by the legs. She swings the lynx over her shoulder like a wet towel.

Muriel, meanwhile, guards the rabid triplets, waving her pistols threateningly. Charlie hurries over, ties them up, and throws their weapons into the sea. Charlie, Frida, and Muriel board their dinghy with Savage Claw, who is still out cold, leaving the lynx's disarmed crew behind on the Nightmare.

Back on the **Anne Bonny**, *they take the lynx below deck. There's a smell of moldy bread and stale water. Frida plops Savage Claw onto the wooden floor. Charlie and Muriel bring over the foot shackles and clap them onto the lynx.*

"Frida, wake her up! Time for questioning," Charlie orders and crosses her arms.

Splash! A bucket of sea water lands in the lynx's face. Snorting, coughing, and spitting, she comes to, extends her claws and tries to grab Charlie. Charlie grins as her enemy is held back at the last moment by the heavy iron chains.

Savage Claw narrows her eyes to slits and hisses: "You'll pay for this!"

"Why are you following us?!" asks Charlie, unmoved. Savage Claw doesn't say a word.

Then Charlie turns to her bear friend and sticks out her paw, "Frida, the nail clippers, please. We'll have to trim the kitten's claws."

"You wouldn't dare!" hisses the lynx, struggling at her chains.

With a broad grin and bright eyes, Charlie walks along under the trees. While she interrogates her enemy in her imagination, she walks deeper and deeper into the forest with a sleepwalker's assurance. Her legs carry her through the ever denser underbrush. But then she stumbles over a stone and peers, surprised, into the darkness. "Where am I? How did I get here?" she asks herself and looks round. Frantically, she wheels round and recognizes the outline of a cave. A bit farther, dim light spills out of the entrance. When she looks again, she sees two amber eyes flashing in the darkness.

An Encounter in the Wolf's Cave

Charlie's heart jumps, and she freezes. Who or what is that? A heatwave jolts through her body, then she breaks out in a cold sweat. "Escape!" she thinks desperately, but her legs won't obey her. She can only watch in horror as the eyes come closer.

Suddenly, hot breath wafts toward her and she feels herself being sniffed about her head and ears. In slow motion, Charlie forces her head up, and her gaze meets long, sharp teeth dancing back and forth before her eyes.

"What are you looking for?!", sounds a menacing growl. Every word softly echoes back and forth between the cave walls.

Charlie crouches down lower. Her mind is empty, fear constricts her throat. She squeezes her eyes shut as if this could make her invisible. Then something cold and wet touches her shoulder. Charlie flinches, grabs at the spot, and feels a wet muzzle. A shrill yip escapes her, and she pulls her paw back. A snarl echoes through the cave, "Go away."

Charlie's legs finally wake up. She takes two steps backward, turns around, runs out of the cave... and trips over a root. Thump! Charlie falls headfirst and remains flat on the ground for a moment with her paws outstretched. All her strength leaves her. "Please, please don't eat me!" she whimpers and struggles to get back onto all fours.

When she straightens herself up, Charlie sees a snowy white she-wolf moving toward her with long, silent strides. Charlie pulls up her scraped knees and sinks her head onto her arms. A sob shakes her entire body.

"Stop crying and go home. It's almost dark," says the wolf, nudging Charlie's side with a paw.

"And which way is home?!" asks Charlie.

The wolf gives her a puzzled look. "Well, wherever you came from."

Charlie lets her gaze wander over the dense, dark branches of the Lost Forest, "But I don't know where I am or how to get home."

"An animal that doesn't watch where it's going, breaking into other people's homes ... pathetic," snorts the wolf.

Now Charlie is seized with rage. She pulls the wolf's head down by the ear and screams, "You don't even have a door! Pathetic yourself, you stupid wolf!"

The wolf yanks her head away and sits down on her hind legs. Puzzled, she rubs her ear with a paw and makes a face.

"You can scream pretty loud for such a small rabbit. Come on, I'll walk with you for a bit."

The wolf starts moving. Charlie's scraped knees are still burning and she has to hurry to keep up. Every time Charlie almost catches up with her, the wolf speeds up a little, staying one step ahead. Light-footed, she moves over roots, stones, and branches.

"It's like she's floating above the forest floor," Charlie thinks, fascinated.

Soon, she can no longer keep up the pace and slows down. Immediately and without looking back, the wolf also slows.

"She notices everything," Charlie thinks and asks aloud, "How do you do that?"

"What?" the wolf replies and trots on.

"All that. The way you move, the way you notice everything."

"That," says the wolf, without looking back, "is the secret of wolves – the wolf's eye. Every young wolf has to practice it for years."

Now Charlie is curious. "The wolf's eye? How does it work?"

"A wolf has to live completely in the moment. She has to see everything, hear everything. There is nothing in her thoughts but the task before her."

"I can do that, too," says Charlie, "you don't have to be a wolf for that. When I'm drawing or in the workshop with Papa, I live in the moment, too, and don't think about anything else."

"Pah!" snorts the wolf, "that's easy. The wolf's eye isn't only for fun things. A wolf can use the wolf's eye even when she's scared, tired, or doesn't like her task. A wolf can decide to use it any time. Wolf's eye on – click – and then she's alert, focused, at one with the task."

Charlie goes quiet, thinking as she tries to keep up.

"Hey, wolf?" she says after a while. "Can you teach me that wolf's eye? It would really come in handy! For school, you know?"

The wolf turns and looks at her disdainfully.

"A rabbit with the wolf's eye? How ridiculous ... You couldn't learn it in a hundred years."

Charlie's cheeks burn. What a mean thing to say!

"You might be able to do the wolf's eye," she mutters, "but you're very unfriendly. That's probably why you're all alone!"

The wolf stops abruptly, bares her teeth in Charlie's direction, and growls. Charlie shrinks back.

"No offense," she says quickly. But the wolf's gaze remains grim.

"Up ahead is the clearing with the old oak tree. From there you can find your way home on your own. Now get out of my forest."

With a sudden movement, the wolf turns around and trots back into the thicket. Charlie's gaze follows her. The wolf disappears into the branches without looking back. It's already dark when Charlie gets home. Mama Rabbit sits on the bench in front of the rabbit house, looking at her watch and into the distance by turns.

Charlie is sure she will get a bad scolding. As a precaution, she pulls back her ears.

But when her mother sees her, she rushes over, wraps her tightly in her arms and exclaims, “There you are at last! I was so worried.”

Now Papa Rabbit pokes his head through the front door, too: “Where have you been, little lady? Your mother was worried sick,” he says. “And dinner’s cold, too!”

Charlie is still out of breath from running the last part of the way home.

“I had detention ... it took a really long time. And then I got lost and ran into a wolf and she didn’t eat me and she can do the wolf’s eye and I want to learn that too.”

Papa Rabbit shakes his head. “Charlie, you and your made-up stories. I’m sure you’ve just been daydreaming again! Now come in, eat something and then off to bed with you.”

No sooner said than done. During dinner, Mama Rabbit strokes Charlie’s arm again and again. And although it’s already late, Charlie persuades her parents to play a game of cards with her before she has to go to bed.

“Wolf’s eye,” Charlie murmurs a little later in the warmth of her bed. She snuggles under her favorite blanket, the one Mama Rabbit made for her, and dreams of striding through the forest – alert, focused, and with sharpened senses.

Charlie Surprises Everyone

Early the next morning, Charlie wakes up before the alarm clock goes off. This morning is different. Charlie feels wide awake. She feels the blanket, soft and warm, against her fur. She hears the birds chirping outside, and as she lifts her nose and sniffs, there's the scent of freshly baked bread.

"Wolf's eye on!" says Charlie silently to herself.

She gets up and goes to her chest of drawers: "put on underwear, put on dress ..." she recites and gazes intently at her clothes. "At one with the task like a wolf!"

In no time at all, Charlie is dressed. She is already clutching her backpack when the alarm clock goes off. "Charlie! Get up!" calls Mama Rabbit from the kitchen.

"Won't she be surprised!" Charlie thinks, taking the stairs two steps at a time and casually sitting down on her chair at the table. Her mother's jaw drops.

Even her father looks up from the newspaper, nods appreciatively, and asks, "What's up with you?"

Mama Rabbit smiles. "How nice that you are ready for school already! Now we can take our time! I'll make us some hot chocolate." Charlie's mouth waters.

A little later, Charlie arrives at the old oak tree. "Ha, first one here!" she thinks and laughs softly. This time, she is the one leaning against the tree trunk, waiting for her friends to arrive.

When she spots Muriel in the distance, she hides behind the tree trunk. Muriel comes waddling up and Charlie jumps out of her hiding place, lunging at her friend and growling like a wolf. Muriel lets out a shrill scream and faints. Startled, Charlie leans over her friend.

"Hey Muriel, it's me, I was just kidding. Wake up!"

With both paws, she tries to prop Muriel up, but her friend is too heavy. Her long duck neck lolls back and forth uncontrollably whenever Charlie tries to lift her.

"What are you doing?" someone grumbles behind Charlie. Frida has arrived and stares at the motionless duck. Without further ado, she grabs Muriel by the neck with her bear paws and shakes her a bit.

"I scared her. And then she just keeled over."

"We'll take care of that right now," Frida says, as she swings the duck over her shoulder and trots off to the duck pond with Charlie in tow.

She takes Muriel from her shoulder, holds her tightly by her webbed feet, and dunks her headfirst into the cold water for a moment.

Coughing and with eyes wide open, Muriel comes to.
"What? Where?" she quacks.
"She's back," Frida grumbles and sets Muriel down.
The duck is still a little wobbly on her feet and staggers slightly to one side. She glares angrily at Charlie. "Don't you ever do that again! Never do that again!"
"Sorry. Are you ok?" says Charlie, stroking her friend's feathers with her paw.
Muriel shakes herself. "I really thought it was the wolf and that he was about to eat me!"
Charlie smiles at her, "It's a she-wolf, and she's not so dangerous. I met her!"
Charlie has a lot to tell her friends. The whole way to school she tells them about her adventure in the Lost Forest.
Just before they arrive at school, Muriel asks: "Hey, aren't you excited about the treasure hunt in the forest? I hope we're in the same group!"
Frida grins, and Charlie also beams at the thought of school today. For the treasure hunt, Mrs. Lynx always hides marbles in the forest behind the school. Equipped with a compass and map, the children run in groups from one hiding place to the next to collect all the marbles. These are counted by Mrs. Lynx at the end.
"You've found all of them. Congratulations!" she says to the class a few hours later. "As a reward, everyone gets a

goody bag with an apple, a fresh bread roll, and some chocolate!"

Refreshed and in a good mood, the three friends make their way home after the treasure hunt. Charlie is still talking about her encounter with the wolf and how she practiced the wolf's eye in the morning. Frida is already a little tired of listening. She mumbles an "aha" and a "hmm" here and there and looks at the mushrooms and stones along the way. Muriel remains silent and waddles slowly behind the others.

After a while, Frida looks back at Muriel and asks, "Hey, what's up?"

Muriel looks down at the ground in embarrassment and kneads her wings. "I was just thinking, well, I was really lucky this morning when you dunked me in the pond," she says. "I could have lost my friendship bracelet. Splash! – in the water and gone."

She casts a furtive glance at Charlie's paw. Charlie follows her friend's gaze. And suddenly, hot and cold shivers run down her spine.

It can't be!

Her friendship bracelet is gone! Thoughts race through her head. "Oh no, how could this have happened! I never take it off! Or did I? Did I put it somewhere? Muriel knows I don't have it on. She's about to get mad. What do I say now?"

Charlie tries to stay calm and not let on that anything is wrong. "Oh, both of you kept your friendship bracelets on today? Weren't you afraid they'd get dirty during the treasure hunt, looking for the marbles?"

Frida shakes her head. "No, I wear mine on my ear. It doesn't get dirty there. And Muriel has it around her neck. But you're right, it's a good thing you didn't put yours on today. Look how dirty your paws are."

Muriel scrutinizes Charlie. "Is that really why you didn't wear it today? If you don't like it, you can say so. I won't get mad."

"No. I love it," Charlie tries to calm her friend, thinking, "I have to find that bracelet. Otherwise, she'll be upset with me for days."

Fortunately, the old oak tree is already in sight and Charlie is able to excuse herself with a quick, "Byyyyyyyyeee, see you tomorrow!"

She once again runs the rest of the way home. When she gets in, she turns the place upside down looking for her friendship bracelet. It has to be here somewhere! And today, of all days, her parents are not home. Charlie pulls open all the drawers, rummages through her closet and her piles of toys, flings all the books off the shelf.

With increasing desperation, she searches in ever more unlikely places: She lifts up the carpet, turns over the sofa cushions, looks in the cutlery drawer, shines the flashlight into the shower drain, and empties the trash can in front of the house, poking around in it with a stick.

But there is no sign of the bracelet anywhere. Finally, Charlie hops back into the house, goes into her room, and jumps up on her bed. There she sits, in the middle of the big mess she's made. Clothes all over the floor, books and toys tossed everywhere, drawers open and their contents scattered.

Finally, she hears the front door swing open. "Hello bunny, we're baaa-aack!" calls Mama Rabbit.

Charlie stomps out of her room, angry that her parents have left her alone today. "Where have you been?" she demands.

"Shopping, like we told you," her father replies, stroking her head. Charlie turns away. Mama Rabbit goes into the kitchen, takes one look at the living room, and drops the shopping bags in shock.

"Herbert! Look at this! We've been burgled!" Papa Rabbit rushes over to look for himself.

"Doesn't look like a break-in to me," he says dryly. "Charlie, was that you?"

"My bracelet is gone! I've looked everywhere for it!" says Charlie with a lump in her throat.

Her mother shakes her head and presses her paw to her chest: “Oh, my tattered turnip! What a mess! We just straightened up everything this morning! Herbert, say something!”

Papa Rabbit looks sternly at Charlie. “When you make a mess, you have to clean it up! Start right now!”

“But my bracelet is gone!” cries Charlie. “I need it tomorrow!” Her voice breaks.

Her father just shakes his head. “It’s no wonder you never find anything in all your chaos,” he scolds. “You’d lose your head if it weren’t screwed on.”

Tears swim in Charlie’s eyes. “Now you’re criticizing me too!” she howls, running to her room.

Before she slams the door, she hears her father complaining, “Why can’t we have a quiet afternoon like a normal family, just for once? I’ll be in the workshop.”

After a few minutes, Charlie hears footsteps in the hallway. The door to her room slowly opens and Mama Rabbit slips inside. She makes her way through the mess and sits down on the bed with Charlie. “What kind of bracelet did you lose, Charlie?” she asks.

“My friendship bracelet from Muriel. She’ll hate me if I’ve lost it ...”

Sniffling, Charlie tells her mother about the day’s events.

"When did you last see it? Did you take it off last night, perhaps?"
Her mother tries to help her, but Charlie just can't think where it could be.
"When you came home from detention last night, you definitely didn't have a bracelet on," her mother muses.
"Then I lost it in the woods and I'll never find it again!" sobs Charlie, burying her head in her mother's fur.
Mama Rabbit hugs Charlie. "Muriel will still be your friend, don't worry."
It's quiet at the table during dinner. Charlie listlessly pokes at her herb lasagna. Papa Rabbit is the first to finish. He puts his plate in the sink and quickly excuses himself. "I'm going back to the workshop – I have to finish something."
"Come on, we'll wash the dishes and then I'll help you tidy up," says Mama Rabbit, putting her paw on Charlie's arm.
Together they tidy the kitchen first, then the living room. Charlie's mother puts on music to make it a little easier for them.

"Now your room, and then we're done," says Mama Rabbit after a while.
Charlie sighs, "Can't I do it tomorrow?"
At that moment, her father walks through the door carrying two wooden boxes. "Since there's so much chaos, we might as well clean it up right," he says, leading the way into Charlie's room. "Look, I made you two big boxes with wheels. We'll put all your toys in one box and your coloring and drawing materials in the other. Just fill them up and push them under the bed. It's quick and makes the room look nice afterwards."
Charlie stands in the middle of the room, looking at the mess in confusion. When Papa puts it that way, it sounds so simple. But right now she has no idea where to start.
"Charlie, find all the toys and throw them in here. I'll help you."
"Find toys," Charlie thinks, "wolf's eye on, be at one with the task." Despite a tired head and a huge mountain of stuff, she sorts through her things quickly.

Her father disappears for a moment and then returns with a snow shovel. "This will make it go even faster," he says with a grin.

The clothes are back in the closet, the books on the shelf, the toys and coloring materials in the boxes under the bed.

Mama and Papa Rabbit put Charlie to bed with a hug and a bedtime story. Now she lies there, staring at the ceiling, wondering how she's going to confess to Muriel tomorrow that she's lost her bracelet. Thinking, "I'd rather be sick tomorrow and stay home," she falls asleep exhausted.

When the alarm clock rings the next morning, Charlie wakes up sweaty and with a pounding heart. During the night, she kept waking up with a start. In her dreams, Muriel broke up their friendship and even Frida abandoned her in disappointment.

"How could I have lost that bracelet? I'm so stupid!" Charlie is angry at herself.

That morning, she doesn't think about the wolf's eye. Her mother has to drag her out of bed. Charlie feels heavy, like a rock. She gets dressed in slow motion while her mother keeps looking at the clock.

"Charlie, you're going to be late," Mama Rabbit reminds her.

Charlie feels her mother's gaze as she chews her cereal sluggishly.

"If you don't leave now, you won't make it in time. Muriel is probably anxious already," Mama Rabbit reminds her again.

Charlie chokes down the last bite, trudges to the front door, turns the handle, and is about to step outside when she sees something lying on the doormat.

She bends down and picks it up in disbelief: her bracelet! Really! How is that possible? It found its way back to her undamaged. Charlie's heart lifts.

But what is that? A single white hair caught in the purple yarn!

"The wolf! She brought it to me!"

Relieved and happy, Charlie runs to the old oak tree.

I'm Going to Get in Trouble!

Charlie runs to the old oak tree so fast that she has to gasp for air. Sweat runs down her back, and she feels dizzy. But there is no sign of Muriel and Frida.

"They left without me!"

Annoyed, Charlie kicks the old oak tree, clenches her fists, and stomps off to school. Just as she dashes across the little bridge, the wind carries the sound of the ringing school bell to her ears.

"I'm going to get in trouble!" Charlie thinks and puts on a sprint. A few minutes later, she storms through the front gate and collides with the handyman, Mr. Boar.

"Watch where you're going!" he grunts at her. "No running in the hallway!"

Finally, Charlie reaches the classroom. She takes a deep breath, pushes the door handle down and, under the stern gaze of Mrs. Lynx, slouches into her seat.

"Did you correct the essays?" asks David, the little badger.

The teacher smiles.

"I did, and I'm very pleased with how well they turned out and how many adjectives you used."

Mrs. Lynx clutches the stack of essays and begins handing them back to the children. "David, very good! Livia, exciting text! Theo, almost two pages, bravo! Frida, your best essay so far, congratulations ..."

Now Mrs. Lynx stops in front of Charlie's desk.

"Charlotte, stay a moment after class, I need to talk to you," she says as she slides the corrected essay onto her desk.

When Charlie notices Muriel peeking at her paper with obvious curiosity, she quickly pulls it to her chest. Another "unsatisfactory" grade! She quickly stuffs the essay into her backpack. Her stomach tightens. With a lump in her throat, she swallows hard.

Mrs. Lynx now turns to the duck. “And finally, you, Muriel: excellent! An excellent text.”

Muriel ruffles her feathers, proudly takes the essay, shows it to Frida, and asks, “What grade did you get?”

Frida grins, holds up her essay and taps her paw on the words “*Very good*” written in bold red next to an ink stamp of a laughing sun.

“Great, Frida!” quacks Muriel. “I even got a crown stamp and an ‘*Excellent*.’ Look at the crown.”

She stretches out her wing toward the bear behind Charlie’s head. The two give each other a high five.

Charlie sits motionless in her chair, staring at her desk, saying nothing. Around her, everyone is cackling, humming, quacking, roaring, and squealing all at the same time.

“All right, everybody, settle down!” shouts Mrs. Lynx through the din.

“You’ve really done a great job! Muriel, you especially. You used 23 adjectives in your essay, more than anyone else. Will you please read your excellent essay to the class?”

“What, me? You want me to read it aloud?” squeals Muriel joyfully.

Mrs. Lynx nods. “Come to the front, please.”

Her chest puffed out with pride, Muriel waddles forward, wagging her tail feathers. She turns to the class, grins, and clears her throat:

"Essay topic: 'This Is Who I Am.'
Describe yourself
using as many adjectives
as possible."

My name is Muriel. That's Irish and means bright, shining sea. I am a ten-year-old duck. I live on a big, lily-covered pond. I live there with my mother and my eight wild and rude little brothers and sisters who still have soft feathers. My last report card said that I am a helpful, dutiful, careful, and diligent student. My mother says that's true, and that I'm responsible because I take care of my brothers and sisters when she has to work at the café. I have not just one but two best friends: bear-strong Frida and daydreamy Charlie. As a friend, I am nice, honest, funny, and not judgmental. But I also have weaknesses. Sometimes I get nervous during tests and lectures. I'd like to be more courageous."

"Bravo!" praises Mrs. Lynx, "a little applause please for our Muriel! Which adjectives did you hear?" the teacher asks the class.

Frida answers. "Bear-strong, hardworking, responsible."

"Very good! Marvin, do you want to say something too?"

"Yes. Lily-covered, nervous, and daydreamy Charlie," the little weasel counts off.

Charlie buries her head in her arms. When will this finally be over?

"Good," says Mrs. Lynx. "But 'Charlie' is not an adjective. Muriel, you can sit down again."

"Uh ... yes, Mrs. Lynx," Muriel stammers, as if she has just woken up from a dream. On the way to her seat, the duck grins at her friends. Frida smiles back and gives her a thumbs-up.

It's one of those school days when Charlie hardly notices anything happening. She sits sullenly and quietly on her chair, occasionally looking out the window or burying her head in her paws. Again and again, she glances at the clock above the door. The hands seem frozen.

In second period, Frida taps her on the shoulder and whispers "I'm sorry." Charlie sighs and doesn't respond.

Twice she is admonished by Mrs. Lynx: "Charlotte, pay attention! Do I have to repeat the question?" She repeats it, but Charlie feels everyone looking at her and does not know the answer.

Finally, the bell rings. The morning is over and Charlie packs up her things at a snail's pace.

Just as she is about to sneak out of the classroom, Mrs. Lynx blocks her way. "Charlotte, I told you that I want to talk to you."

Frida turns to her. "Shall we wait for you?"

"No, it's okay, I can go home by myself," Charlie mutters and goes back into the classroom. Mrs. Lynx sits down

at her desk and pulls out a chair for Charlie.
"Sit down. Charlotte, I'm concerned about your essay. You were the only one to get an unsatisfactory. I just don't understand! After all, we've been studying adjectives for two weeks. The assignment was easy. Describe yourself using as many trait words as possible. Charlotte, you hardly used any and wrote almost nothing about yourself. And your spelling was a disaster! I don't want to give you bad grades, but you really need to try harder and concentrate more. Today you didn't pay attention at all. You're friends with Muriel. Maybe she can help you?"

Charlie sinks down in her chair, fights back tears, and swallows hard. She sees Mrs. Lynx as if through a thick veil of mist, the teacher's voice seems to come from far away. Charlie hears the blood rushing in her ears, and heat spreads throughout her body. The teacher talks and talks. Her words drum against Charlie and swirl around in her head.

"Charlotte! Wake up! You're not listening again!" says Mrs. Lynx, tapping Charlie's shoulder with her paw.

Charlie shakes off the teacher's paw and glares at her. "I am trying! But I always do everything wrong and no one is ever happy with me!" Tears are streaming down her face.

Mrs. Lynx moves her chair a little closer.
"We all just want to help you. But you have to try a bit harder."
"How?" Charlie sputters, crosses her arms, and turns away.

"You are actually smart. You just need to pay more attention," says Mrs. Lynx.

"But I can't do any better! My head is always doing something else! And I'm always supposed to pay attention! When I get up and get dressed, when I'm in class, when I do my homework, when we practice dictation, and when I have to clean up. But nobody tells me *how* to pay attention!"

Mrs. Lynx leans back in her chair, gazes thoughtfully out the window, scratches her ears.

"Can I go now?" mumbles Charlie, wiping the tears from her face with her paw.

"Yes, see you tomorrow," Mrs. Lynx murmurs and sighs.

When Charlie pushes open the the schoolhouse door, a cool breeze swirls through her whiskers. She takes a deep breath and steps outside. After she's taken the first few steps, heavy, cold raindrops start patting down her fur. As she crosses the schoolyard, she looks back and sees Mrs. Lynx standing at the classroom window. The teacher lifts a paw and waves to her.

SCHOOL

Wandering Around the Lost Forest

Raindrops pound onto the ground, quickly turning it wet and muddy. Charlie starts to run. She hurries across the bridge, dodges puddles, and repeatedly wipes rainwater from her eyes. "My school stuff's getting wet!" flashes through her mind.

She swerves and ducks to shelter under the trees on the edge of the Lost Forest. Here, the treetops are so dense that they hardly let in any light or rain. Charlie shakes off the water and sits down on a moss-covered rock. She takes off her backpack and peers inside. "Just in time," she thinks as she looks at her papers and books. They've already got a little damp on top and are starting to ripple. She sets the backpack on the ground and wraps her arms around her knees. She starts rubbing her damp fur, trying to chase away the cold.

Shivering, she looks up into the thick canopy of leaves and listens to the tapping of the raindrops. As she sits under the trees, she begins to rip moss from the rock and crumble it onto the ground. "Stupid Mrs. Lynx, I'd love to ..." she thinks as she plucks out an especially big tuft and escapes into her dream world.

"Ow! You'll regret that!" Savage Claw screams and yanks at her chains.
Charlie looks disdainfully at the tuft of fur she's plucked from her enemy and blows it into her face like a kiss. The lynx's eyes narrow to slits.
"And now," Charlie says, "answer my question:
Why are you following us?"
"Tell her, tell her!" quacks Muriel, waving her guns.
The lynx's claw shoots forward, pointing at Charlie:
"Because there's not room enough for both you and me on my ocean!"
Charlie crosses her arms and looks down at her enemy from above.
"Your ocean? Ha! You don't even have a ship, and your crew's glad to be rid of you. You can stay down here and smell your own stench."
Charlie, Muriel, and Frida turn around, climb the stairs, and let the hatch slam shut. They can still hear their prisoner rattling her chains and yelling after them.*
Muriel flutters around Charlie: "What are we going to do?
What are we going to do with her?"
Charlie adjusts her hat. "You go back to the crow's nest.
And Frida: You set the sails. We'll set course for Skull Island and chuck the kitty ashore there."
Frida lifts her snout into the wind. "What's that funny smell?"

* Hatch: opening on a ship that can be closed with a board on hinges.

Charlie sniffs, turns her head and looks straight into two large amber eyes. Startled, she tumbles backward off the rock and lands on the soft forest floor.

"Well, well, look who's wandering around my forest again!" says the wolf, nudging Charlie back to her feet with her muzzle and smirking.

"Very funny," Charlie grumbles, brushing moss and pine needles out of her fur.

"Now, now. Such a grumpy little bunny." The wolf shakes her head and sits on her hind legs. "Where I come from, you would have been eaten a long time ago."

Charlie looks at her with wide eyes. "Then you really are from the north? Do you really eat other animals there? My friend Frida told me that."

The wolf's eyes darken. "That's not a story for children."

"But is it true?" Charlie wants to know.

"You are the oddest and nosiest rabbit I have ever met."

Charlie lets her ears droop and looks down at the ground.

"That's no reason to be sad, is it?" says the wolf.

"Yes it is!" retorts Charlie, "Yes it is! Because everyone thinks I'm odd and a daydreamer. And because I can't do anything right!"

The wolf smiles at her. "You can dream. That's rare."

Charlie just snorts. "That's exactly why everyone thinks I'm stupid. Everyone's always telling me: *Stop dreaming! Pay attention! Concentrate!* And now you're at it as well!"

She drops down on all fours, licks her whiskers, and mimics the wolf: "Where I come from, you would have been eaten a long time ago!"

"Awoohoohoohaha!" The wolf emits such a funny mix of howling and laughter that Charlie can't help but laugh too.

"You're hilarious," the wolf says, wiping a tear of laughter from the corner of her eye with her paw.

"What's your name, anyway?"

"Charlie."

"I'm Sakiba. And as for dreaming, you just have to find the right moment for it – then it's valuable."

Charlie steps a little closer to the wolf and sits cross-legged in front of her. "Why valuable?" she wants to know.

"Many wolves practice the wolf's eye until they forget how to dream. They stay focused on their task, seeing only what is in front of their faces, hearing only what the leader of the pack commands them to do, and forgetting who they are. Dreams reveal what could be. They are the gateway to new ideas, to your desires and feelings. They lead you to solutions that no one has thought of before."

Charlie perks up her ears. "Really?"

"Yes. A wolf doesn't lie. Daydreaming is valuable, at the right time. And the wolf's eye is valuable, at the right time."

"And when is the right time?" Charlie wants to know.

"It is wise to ask that question," says the wolf, "think about that for a while."

With a smile, Sakiba turns away and disappears into the dense forest. Astonished, Charlie follows her with her eyes though the wolf can no longer be seen.

"I didn't even get a chance to thank her for leaving the bracelet at my door," she thinks.

The forest is quiet. The rain has stopped. Charlie gets up, grabs her backpack and sets off for home.

Puddles have formed everywhere. Charlie takes a running start and jumps over the first, the second, the third, and lands in the fourth with a big “splash”.

"Oh no," she thinks as she looks down at herself. A brown, muddy mess is dripping off her dress. Suddenly she starts to giggle. She's just about to hop over another puddle when she sees her mother hurrying toward her from a distance.

Charlie waves and runs toward her. At the last moment, she calls out, “Mama, look!”

With a giant leap, she jumps over the three-foot long puddle that is between her and her mother. Splash!

“Charlie! Are you nuts? You’re not five years old anymore!”

Stunned, with soaking wet clothes and a mud-splattered face, Mama Rabbit stares at her daughter:

"And where have you been?"

Embarrassed, Charlie lowers her eyes. She's knee deep in the puddle. "Sorry ... I had to stay behind at school. Mrs. Lynx wanted to talk to me and then it rained really hard and I had to take shelter so that my school things wouldn't get wet and then ..."

"I see," says her mother, lifting Charlie's backpack with an outstretched paw, watching the brown puddle water drip off.

"Honestly, Mama! And then I met the wolf again."

Mama Rabbit shakes her head and clucks her tongue. "Oh Charlie, you and your imagination."

She puts a paw on her daughter's back. "Mrs. Lynx called me earlier and told me about your essay and your conversation."

Charlie looks up at her mother. "I know I got another bad grade."

"That's not why Mrs. Lynx called. She said she'd been thinking about your conversation. She sensed that you aren't feeling too good. Then I told her how long we always sit together doing your homework."

Charlie hops along silently beside her mother, scowling as she kicks a pebble into a puddle.

"Mrs. Lynx doesn't want you to have to spend the whole afternoon doing homework every day. She suggested that going forward you should just do half an hour and then go play."

Charlie turns her head to her mother in disbelief. Wide-eyed, she reaches for Mama Rabbit's hand. A warm feeling flows through her body.

The Apology

As Charlie scrubs the last crust of mud from her fur in the shower upstairs, the sun starts to shine through the bathroom window. Her stomach growls loudly. Downstairs in the kitchen, Papa Rabbit is putting his famous Papa Pie in the oven: vegetables in flaky pastry.

When Charlie has eaten the last piece, she leans back and rubs her belly in satisfaction. Mama Rabbit says, "today we'll do it the way Mrs. Lynx and I discussed: only a half hour of homework, and you can take a short break every ten minutes. Do you want to start now or rest a little longer?"

Charlie breathes a sigh of relief that she won't have to study all afternoon. "I'd rather get it over with now, so I can draw later!"

She puts her folders and books on the kitchen table. They're still a little damp.

"It's best if you write in pencil so it doesn't get all smeared," Papa Rabbit suggests as he clears the table.

Mama Rabbit sits down with her and puts a big alarm clock on the table. Together, they go through the homework and discuss what Charlie wants to start with.

"Are you ready? Do you know what to do? Ok, then here we go," says Mama, starting the clock.

"Ok, full concentration! Wolf's eye on! At one with the task!" Charlie says to herself and reads the instructions on her English worksheet: *Underline all adjectives*.

“Underline the adjectives,” Charlie mumbles and makes a start while her mother has a coffee and browses through her magazine.

During her first break, Charlie listens to her favorite song; during the second, she runs around the house three times. Then she starts working on the math problems.

When the alarm clock rings for the last time, Charlie briefly finishes calculating.

“You can stop there. That’s enough work for today,” says Mama Rabbit.

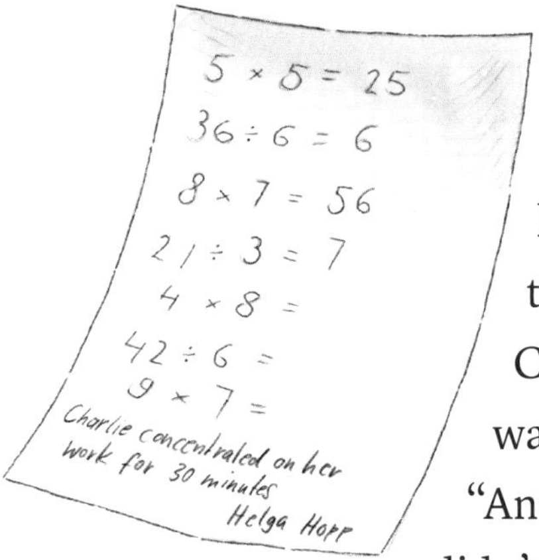

Charlie puts the pencil aside while her mother looks at the worksheet.

“Wow, bunny! You’re more than halfway through. You’ve never been this fast and focused before.”

Charlie’s heart jumps a little, and a warm feeling spreads through her body.

“And Mrs. Lynx won’t get mad at me if I didn’t finish everything?”

Mama Rabbit shakes her head, “Don’t worry.” With her pencil, she writes a note for Mrs. Lynx on the worksheet.

As Charlie is packing her backpack for the next day at school with her mother, the doorbell rings.

Mama Rabbit goes to the door.

“Hello you two, I didn’t know you were coming!” she says. “Perfect timing. Charlie just finished her homework. Come in!”

Frida squeezes through the narrow door of the rabbit house with a little groan, and Muriel flutters in behind her.

"What are you doing here?" Charlie asks, surprised.

"We came to apologize," Frida says, swaying from one foot to the other.

"Because we left without you this morning," Muriel mutters, wringing her wings. "And because you did so badly on your essay and we didn't help you feel better."

Frida adds, "We're really sorry. We should at least have waited for you after class when Mrs. Lynx wanted to talk to you."

"That's ok," Charlie mumbles.

Muriel wiggles her tail feathers excitedly.

"We made something for you to make up for it! We made it ourselves!"

She struts into the living room with long strides. Frida walks behind her, gingerly stepping around the furniture, and only just catching a floor lamp she almost knocked down with her flank. The three friends make themselves comfortable in the living room. Frida sits down carefully on the sofa, which creaks alarmingly, and pulls a large scroll of paper from her bag. Muriel unties the bow and spreads the paper on the table with a sweep of her wings.

Charlie bends over the artwork and beams at her friends.

"Thank you!"

Our best friend
Charlie

courageous

funny

always there for us

sweet

honest

can draw very w

always has good ideas

it is never boring with her

We like you very much

Then she looks at the drawing a little longer and giggles.

"Your ears got a bit long," Muriel apologizes and strokes the picture with her feathers.

Frida grins. "That's the best we could do. You're better at drawing and decorating."

Charlie shrugs her shoulders. "I think it's wonderful!"

Carefully, she picks up the poster with her paws, like a treasure. "Let's hang this up in my room right now!"

The Lily Pond

The sunshine lures the three friends outside. They decide to go swimming in the lily pond next to the school. Marvin Weasel and David Badger from their class are already there, wrestling and yelling in the water, and dunking each other's heads under.

"No yelling here!" shouts Mr. Boar, the handyman, who is sunning himself next to the dock with his wife. She shakes her head, rolls her eyes, and flips through her magazine in exasperation.

"Last one in is a rotten egg!" shouts Frida to her friends and runs off. With a deafening roar, she jumps off the little dock into the pond, splashing and spraying water everywhere.

"No splashing in the pond!" yells Mr. Boar, waving his claw in admonishment. His wife gasps, her bristly fur dripping and her magazine hanging down like a wet rag.

"Oh sorry, very sorry, sorry" Muriel quacks as she slides carefully into the water.

Complaining loudly and shaking their heads, Mr. and Mrs. Boar pack up their things and wander off. Charlie can still hear Mrs. Boar grumbling from afar: "You want to enjoy one single quite evening in the sun and then this. That never would have happened in my day! Kids these days simply have no respect."

Charlie grins and dives headfirst into the pond to join her friends. After playing tag in the water, diving for pebbles, and giving each other marks for the craziest and funniest dives, the friends lie down together in the sun and let their fur and feathers dry.

"Oh no," Frida suddenly whispers as she rolls onto her stomach. Charlie looks around and spots the three swans from Frida's ballet class strutting down the path one after the other: beautiful, radiant, with craned necks and all three elegantly in step. As if on cue, all three lift a wing in unison and wave.

"Frida, they're coming over here," Muriel whispers to her friend and nudges her in the side.

The swan girls float over.

"Hello Frida!" the first one says, smiling at the bear.

"Why don't you come to ballet practice anymore?" asks the second.

Frida mutters something about the new ballet teacher, Mrs. Peacock, without looking at the swans.

"Oh, Frida, we miss you so much! You absolutely must come back!" says the third, while the others nod eagerly.

Muriel sits up and folds her wings. "Your Mrs. Peacock doesn't want Frida around anymore."

The swans tilt their heads and look at Frida in surprise.

"How mean of her! Don't let her put you down! We need you for the performance."

"I don't know. I'll think about it," Frida grumbles, rubbing a reed stalk back and forth between her claws.

"The performance is only six weeks away. Please, come back soon!" the swans plead, as they wave goodbye.

The Wolf's Eye and Daydreams

"Shall we get an ice cream?" Muriel suggests, and the three friends set off toward the ice cream parlor in the village. Before long, they are sitting by the fountain, enjoying their ice creams: Frida licks her five scoops of honey ice cream with a big smile, and Charlie's mouth puckers with pleasure from her extra sour lemon-basil ice cream.

"Are you sure you don't want to try it? It's delicious!" Muriel asks for the third time, waving her waffle cone with snail slime ice cream under Charlie's nose.
Charlie shakes her head in disgust and Frida grimaces: "I can smell it all the way over here, that's enough for me."
Charlie dangles her hind legs against the rough stone wall of the fountain. "Oh, by the way, Frida" she asks, smacking her lips, "about the swans earlier. They really want you back. Don't you think ..."
Frida growls. "No! If that stupid Mrs. Peacock thinks I don't fit into the group, then I won't go. Can we talk about something else now?"
In silence, the friends watch Mr. and Mrs. Boar who are now sitting at a table in front of the ice cream parlor. The sundae between them is so high that they have to tilt their heads to look at each other.
Mr. Boar uses a big soup spoon to push an entire ice cream scoop with whipped cream into his wife's snout. She smacks her lips, grunting contentedly, and keeps leaning over the tabletop to scratch her husband's bristly fur. The three friends nudge each other and cover their grins with their paws and wings.
"I ran into the wolf again after school, by the way. She gave me quite a fright," Charlie starts to tell the others about her encounter. Frida and Muriel listen intently.

"… And she said I should think for a while about when dreaming is useful, and then she just took off. Why did she just leave like that?"

At that moment, Mr. Boar yells over to them: "That fountain is not for loitering!"

Charlie, Frida, and Muriel roll their eyes, but get up all the same. It's time to go home anyway. On the way, they eagerly discuss when the wolf's eye is valuable and when daydreaming is valuable.

The next morning, they meet on their way to school a little earlier than usual. Charlie shows her friends where she met the wolf the day before. There, on the edge of the Lost Forest, next to the moss-covered rock, they tack a note for Sakiba onto a spruce tree:

Wolf's Eye

When I have the wolf's eye, I am at one with the task. I focus on the task with all my senses and I am fully absorbed. I don't let myself be distracted by anything or anyone.

This is valuable when:

... I study, do homework, take a test, or complete a task.

... I have to listen.

... I clean up or work on some difficult problem.

... I have to do several things in a row without forgetting anything (e.g., when I have to get dressed, eat breakfast, and brush my teeth in the morning and don't have much time; when I want to take home from school everything I need for homework; or when I make my weekly schedule at school).

Daydreaming

When I daydream, I let my thoughts wander. I detach myself from the here and now and dive into my imagination.

This is valuable when:

... I am stuck on a problem and need new ideas.

... I have lots of time and want to relax.

... I want to do something creative, for example, draw something or write a story.

... I want to keep myself from forgetting something by picturing it in my mind exactly, like in a photograph or a movie.

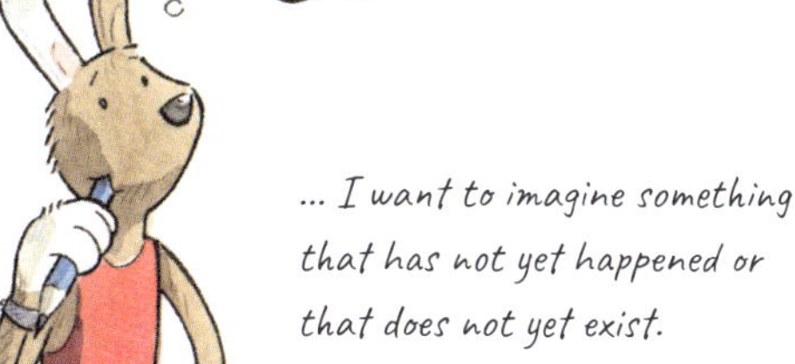

... I want to imagine something that has not yet happened or that does not yet exist.

Charlie finds it hard to pay attention at school. Her thoughts keep wandering off to the wolf. "Has she seen the poster yet? I hope she doesn't think what we wrote is stupid! I wonder if she likes the pictures. Will she answer?"

When the bell rings at the end of class, Charlie has already packed her backpack and urges her friends to hurry.

Charlie and Frida run ahead, Muriel waddles along behind. "Wait! Not so fast! Wait for me!" she quacks, gasping for air.

Finally, the three arrive at the edge of the Lost Forest.

The poster is gone! But what is that lying there on the moss-covered rock under a little stone? An envelope with "Charlie" written on it in beautiful calligraphy. With a pounding heart, she opens the envelope. She skims the lines and smiles at her friends with shining eyes.

"What does it say? Let us read it too!" quacks Muriel as she runs around Charlie in circles. Frida gently pulls the letter out of Charlie's paw and reads it aloud with a serious expression:

Invitation to Wolf Training

Start: Monday after school

Meeting place: Here

Be on time!

Sakiba

Wolf Training

Charlie lies in bed on Sunday night, eagerly anticipating Monday. Just one more night to sleep, then wolf training begins! In the moonlight, Charlie looks at the caravel* that Uncle Louis gave her. She smiles.

"Sleep now, you have to be in good shape tomorrow!" she thinks as she tosses and turns.

All of a sudden, a distant howl sounds through her window.

"Ahhwooooo!"

"Good night, wolf," she mumbles and falls asleep.

The next day, as Charlie walks across the little bridge with her friends after school, she feels her heart pounding and senses Muriel's nervous gaze. For the fifth time, Muriel asks her the same question: "And you're really sure – quite sure – that she won't eat you? The wolf?"

Frida intervenes. "If she wanted to eat Charlie, she would have done it already."

But Muriel babbles on excitedly. "Are you really sure you don't want us to come with you? For protection. We could protect you!"

* Caravel: a sailing ship with two to four masts.

She dances like a little boxer and flaps her wings.
Frida and Charlie smile at each other in amusement.

"Come on, Muriel, let's go," says Frida as the three of them arrive at the edge of the Lost Forest. Then she smothers Charlie in a big bear hug, "Good luck."

Muriel spreads her wings, too, and whispers, "You'll have to tell us everything in detail! Everything!"

Charlie nods and presses her cheek to the duck's.

Then Charlie runs into the Lost Forest. Dead twigs snap under her paws. The smell of moss, sap, and soil is in the air. It gets darker and darker. Charlie's quints until her eyes adjust to the dim light. There she is! Sakiba is enthroned majestically on the mossy rock and fixes Charlie with her amber eyes.

Charlie's body tingles, her heart pounding against her ribcage, "What do I do now? What do I say?" Sakiba has already got up and slides off the rock in one fluid motion. "Ready?" she asks.

"Ready!"

The wolf tilts her head and looks earnestly at Charlie. "First, a wolf must be fully present. Then she needs to sharpen her senses."

Sakiba points to the rock and asks Charlie to sit down on it. Charlie jumps up in two leaps and takes a seat, cross-legged.

Sakiba continues, "Take a moment to arrive fully in the here and now. Concentrate on your body.

Where do you feel contact with the ground? How does the rock you are sitting on feel? Where does the moss touch your fur? Open up your senses and perceive everything in every last detail ...
It may help if you close your eyes*. Now let your attention focus on your hind paws. Notice what you feel, how warm or cold they are ... What do you feel when you slowly let your attention move upwards? To your knees, along your thighs ... continue up to your belly... stay there for a moment and feel how your belly rises and falls as you breathe ... Let your attention continue moving up to your chest .... What do your shoulders feel like ...? Your front legs ...? What are your front paws resting on? Continue moving your attention up to your neck .... Up to your head .... Notice small details: What does your tongue feel like? Where does it press against your front teeth? Go slowly. Take your time. Now you can sense every fiber of your body, from your paws to the tips of your ears."
Charlie feels her body like never before.
It feels like a warm, comforting wave is flowing through her.
"The wind is tickling my whiskers," she giggles.

* You can join Sakiba's wolf training right now if someone can read the next couple of pages to you. To do so, close your eyes. Or fix your gaze on a spot in the distance, if that's more comfortable.

"That's good, now you're completely in the present," Sakiba whispers. "Now pay attention only to your breath. Breathe in through your nose ... and out ... in ... and out ... in ... and out. When thoughts bubble up, you can just let them move on like clouds in the sky and focus on your breathing again. Where do you feel your breathing most? Where does it move your body? In ... and out ...

Now let's sharpen your senses. First, focus on your nose. What do you smell?"

Charlie, with her eyes still closed, sticks her nose in the air. She sniffs. Her nose twitches. She perceives the smell of the wolf, sharp, harsh, and spicy. Soon other scents mingle: the warm forest floor, the musty smell of decaying leaves. She even thinks she can smell a mushroom.

"The forest is full of smells," Charlie marvels.

"Yes, if you take your time to smell them," says Sakiba, her voice low.

"Now we'll train your hearing. Keep your eyes closed and pay attention only to what you hear. Every little sound."

Charlie sharpens her ears. At first, the forest seems quite still. She almost gets bored.

"Concentrate ... what do you hear?" she says quietly to herself.

There, the crack of a branch breaking off. And isn't that a cuckoo that she hears far away in the distance? Charlie points her ears in all directions.

Now she hears the babbling of the brook, the wind rustling through the leaves, her own breath, a bumblebee's buzzing.

"The forest is full of sounds," Charlie marvels.

"Yes, when you're still enough," murmurs Sakiba. "Now your eyes. Open them and look around. Describe to me what you see."

Charlie opens her eyes. Everything seems sharper and clearer to her than usual. The surroundings, smells, sounds, her body: She is completely present and completely at one with herself. She looks around in the forest and lists what she sees: a pine cone, a toadstool, a rotting crooked branch, roots, an abandoned bird's nest...

Sakiba circles the rock.

"That was the first lesson. A wolf must learn to focus on a single thing. On what she hears, sees, senses – or on a single task. Practice that. For a week."

And with that, the wolf disappears into the forest. Charlie focuses her eyes and ears on Sakiba until she is no longer in sight or earshot, then she heads back home.

Tuesday, Wednesday, Thursday – Charlie practices what Sakiba taught her all week. She sits on stones, lies in the grass, practices alone, and shows Muriel and Frida how to focus their minds on a single thing.

Charlie listens to Frida's long, deep breaths, even as Muriel keeps interrupting, "I'm done! What's next?"

On Thursday, Charlie sets herself a difficult task. She sits down in the kitchen before doing her homework, closes her eyes and sharpens her senses. "How does my body feel? From my paws to the tips of my ears? Where do I feel contact with the chair? Breathe in ... breathe out ... What do I smell? What do I hear?"

She opens her eyes again and looks around the room. Then she breathes deep into her belly and out again, says to herself "Wolf's eye on! Go!" She starts the alarm clock and dives into the first assignment. Today, she doesn't even notice her mother entering the kitchen. She only looks up when Mama Rabbit places a plate of carrot chips in front of her, smiles, and says, "Charlie, time for a break!"

Find Me!

"I hope she's there," thinks Charlie as she delves into the Lost Forest the next Monday.

But she's not. The mossy rock is empty! There is no sign of Sakiba anywhere. Charlie leans against the cold stone and waits. She draws circles on the forest floor with her hind legs.

"Where is she? Or did she say that we are not meeting today?"

Charlie grabs a pine cone and throws it against a gnarled tree trunk. It bounces off the bark and lands on the soft forest floor with a dull thump.

Oh, wait, what's that? Charlie squints. Someone has carved something into the tree trunk!

Charlie steps closer, and as she reads her eyes sparkle:

"Just you wait, Sakiba, I'll find you," she says with a grin.

She perks up her ears and listens.

She lifts her nose into the air and sniffs. She turns her wolf's eye deliberately and alertly onto the bushes, the ground, the rocks, the branches. There! A freshly broken twig! Charlie examines it, scrutinizing everything near it.

Behind a fallen tree trunk, she finds a paw print.

"Aha! She jumped over that!"

And what is that on the bush over there? A tuft of white fur!

Charlie discovers more clues, but then Sakiba's trail suddenly ends. Charlie strains her eyes and examines every detail. Nothing!

"Don't forget your other senses!" she thinks and sniffs in all directions.

Suddenly, an acrid, pungent smell assaults her nose. She follows it and discovers another clue.

"Did Sakiba really ...?!"

Ha! Another paw print! The trail leads Charlie out of the Lost Forest.

"Funny, there's the old oak tree right ahead!" Charlie peers out from the underbrush – and sees something white and bushy peeking out from behind the trunk. She runs to the tree and yells, "Gotcha!"

Quick as a flash, Sakiba turns to Charlie and looks her up and down.

"I see you've sharpened your senses," the wolf says, nodding her approval. "You are ready for the second lesson."

Charlie's heart leaps. She proudly tells Sakiba that she's been practicing the wolf's eye all week – even for homework!

"But it doesn't work at school. Mrs. Lynx scolded me again this morning for not listening."

The wolf smiles. "You learn quickly, but you have to be patient. Wolves practice for years until they master the wolf's eye in every situation."

"Will you give me lesson two now?" Charlie wants to know.

"Lesson two!" says Sakiba with a serious face."Wolves stay focused on their task and never lose sight of their goal."

Charlie twirls her whiskers thoughtfully with her paw.

"Focus on your task, don't lose sight of the goal," she murmurs.

Sakiba gives her a searching look. "Try it out, tomorrow at school. After that, we'll meet back here."

Just at that moment, Muriel comes waddling across the meadow by the duck pond.

"Hey, Muriel!" exclaims Charlie. Finally, she can introduce Muriel to Sakiba!

"This is one of my best friends," Charlie says and reaches out to nudge the wolf, but her paw only waves past the empty space already vacated by Sakiba.

Charlie and Muriel sit down under the oak tree, and Charlie tells the duck the second lesson of wolf training: Focus on your task and don't lose sight of your goal.

"That's good! I do something like that too! That's really good!" Muriel bursts out as she claps her wings excitedly. "Tomorrow at school, I'll show you how I do it!

Sakiba's Secret

Screeeech! Mrs. Lynx's claws scrape across the blackboard, leaving more thin grooves. The students flinch and quiet down immediately. The teacher writes the new lesson topic on the board: "Pond and stream." Charlie has her chin propped up on her paw and is looking out the window, lost in thought.

Suddenly, Muriel nudges her in the ribs. "Now! Eyes on the blackboard! Ears up! Take notes! After the lesson, I want to know what Mrs. Lynx explained!" she quacks softly.

Charlie shakes off her daydream and whispers, "Yes! Don't lose sight of the goal. Focus on the task!"

Muriel beams and winks at her.

"Quiet you two!" hisses Mrs. Lynx, knitting her eyebrows.

Charlie lowers her head, opens the notebook, writes the topic at the top of the page, and fixes her gaze on Mrs. Lynx.

A little later, the teacher puts a worksheet on each student's desk. Charlie plucks at her friendship bracelet, looks up in the air, and doesn't even notice that the others have begun writing.

That's when Muriel's wing pokes her in the ribs again. "Eyes on the page, read the task. Don't lose sight of the goal."

Charlie jolts. She slides all the way forward onto the edge of her chair, sits up straight, and turns on the wolf's eye.

She carefully reads the assignment and completes one task after the other.
"Phew, I did it! That was really exhausting!" she thinks as she finishes the worksheet and rubs her eyes.
Finally, the bell rings. Charlie is about to leave the classroom when Mrs. Lynx calls her name. She flinches: "Oh no, what did I do now?" she thinks.
But what is that on Mrs. Lynx' face? A smile?
Yes, indeed.
"You paid careful attention to the first lesson today. Keep it up," purrs the teacher before turning away to wipe the blackboard.
Somehow the school day goes by faster than usual for Charlie. Afterwards, she walks home with her friends, happy.
Muriel and Frida say goodbye at the old oak tree.
Charlie makes herself comfortable on a root and nibbles on the apple left over from break. As soon as her friends are out of sight, Sakiba appears from the bushes at the edge of the woods.
Charlie proudly recounts what happened, "And totally wolf-like, I listened! And even Mrs. Lynx noticed! But I only made it through first period. It was so exhausting!"
The wolf nods. "Yes, the wolf's eye is like a muscle. When you use it, you get tired. But the more you use it, the stronger it gets. Eventually, it becomes easy."

Charlie sinks back into the grass, rests her head on a paw and looks at the clouds. Sakiba sits down in the shade of the oak tree.

"That one looks like a turtle," Charlie says. "And this one looks like a giant ship!"

Sakiba looks up, straining her eyes. "The clouds just look like clouds to me. Where do you see a ship?"

"You have to use the rabbit's eye," Charlie says, laughing.
"Hey, Sakiba?" She hesitates briefly and clears her throat.
"Frida says wolves live in packs. Where is your family?"
The wolf stares past her into space, her jaw set,
teeth gnashing.
"They're up north," she eventually forces out through gritted teeth.
"Do you ever visit them?" Charlie persists.
Sakiba turns a steely gaze onto her. "I don't belong there. And they'd kill me if they found me."

On Skull Island

"They'd kill me if they found me."
Sakiba's words reverberate in Charlie's head.
The clouds float across the sky.
"Don't you have to get home?" Sakiba asks.
"I'm meeting Papa in the village for lunch," Charlie replies.
The two go their separate ways, having agreed to meet again at the old oak tree the following Monday.
On the way to the restaurant, Charlie passes the beaver dam.
The water glistens beautifully in the sun, and she smiles to herself: Dreams and reality melt together sometimes.
Charlie dives into her dream.

"Drop anchor and ready the dinghy! We're going ashore!" roars Charlie.*
In front of them lies Skull Island. Rugged cliffs tower high into the sky. Palm trees line the beach. The sea is calm and clear.
Tied up and scowling, Savage Claw is hauled into the dinghy.
Charlie adjusts her own hat and cutlass and sticks a dagger in her boot.

* Dinghy: a small rowboat carried on a bigger ship.

When everyone is onboard, Frida works the pulley and launches the craft into the water. She grabs the oars and sets course for the beach.

"Look at the fish!" Muriel chatters.

"There! There's a whole school by the coral reef. Even a lionfish!"

The rowboat slides onto the sandy beach.

"Beautiful!" marvels Muriel. "Really beautiful!"

She looks at the lynx. "It's not so bad here."

"You have no idea what this place is!" hisses Savage Claw, clenching her paws into fists.

But Muriel continues to babble blithely, "Coconuts! Come on, let's go collect some. Coconuts are so delicious!"

"We could take some fresh water, too,"

Frida grumbles, nudging Savage Claw in front of her.

"All right," Charlie says. "We'll tie her to a palm tree up ahead by the rocks and go search for provisions."

As they continue toward the rocks, something pokes Charlie's foot through the sole of her boot, "Ouch!" she cries. "What's that?"

"Bones," retorts Savage Claw, "look around!"

And indeed! There are piles of bones all around the rocks: ribs, skulls of various animals, jawbones, thigh bones.

"Baboom. Baboompoompoom. Baboom. Baboompoompoom."

Suddenly from all around, drums start beating, getting faster and faster.

Frida shakes herself. "What is that?"

"Charlie, let's get out of here," Muriel stammers.

As suddenly as they started up, the drums fall silent. A shrill scream makes all four of them flinch. Charlie draws her cutlass. Frida pulls a young palm tree from the ground and holds it in her paws like a club. They hear a rustling in the trees. On a low cliff, small stones come loose and trickle down. Something gray flashes between two bushes. The pirates look around in alarm.

In one fell swoop, a troop of baboons descends on the rocks around them. They pull back their lips and bare long, sharp teeth. They screech, roar, and bark. Faces smeared with white and red warpaint look down on Charlie and her friends with sinister expressions.

The baboons beat their spears on the rocks and shout: "Meat! Meat! Flesh!"

On the highest rock, the leader sits majestically on his red rump. A chain of bird skulls is draped around his neck.

"Welcome to my island! You may stay for dinner!" he barks, laughing uproariously. All the other baboons join in.

"Untie me! You'll never make it without my help!" hisses Savage Claw. Without thinking, Charlie whips her cutlass down and cuts the bonds.

Muriel's beak chatters, her wings and knees tremble and shake.

"Bring me food!" the leader screeches, rattling his skull chain. The baboons leap down from the rocks. A spear whizzes toward Charlie and her friends. Frida swings up the palm tree, blocking the spear just in time. It sticks in the wood, vibrating.
"Catch!" cries Frida, pulling the spear out of the trunk and tossing it over to the lynx.
With mouths agape, the baboons rush at the pirates. Charlie ducks and rolls under the thrusting spears, splintering them with her cutlass. Muriel has taken refuge in a palm tree with a few powerful flaps of her wings. Shrieking wildly and with eyes wide open, she throws coconuts from above at the baboons climbing the tree. "Clonk, plonk!" she hits them right on their skulls one after another. Stunned, they fall from the tree like overripe fruit.

Frida thrashes the enemies with her palm tree. Baboons are thrown through the air in all directions and land on sand, stones, and piles of bones. But there are too many! More and more of them crowd around Frida.

One jumps on her back and bites her in the shoulder. Frida roars, grabs the baboon and catapults it into the advancing troop.
Savage Claw twirls her spear, hitting shins, butts, and arms, striking fast as lightning.

The baboons around Savage Claw growl and groan, but don't let go. A stick catches the lynx on the forehead. Dazed, she staggers backward and falls. Then a spear whizzes toward her eyes. Clang! Charlie deflects it with her cutlass at the last moment. It bores into the sand right next to Savage Claw's ear. The lynx rolls to one side, grabs the dagger from Charlie's boot, and kicks another baboon.

The fight rages on. Charlie and Frida stand back-to-back and desperately fend off the spears. Muriel shrieks in fear. Just then Savage Claw dives behind a bush and quietly steals away .

"Coward!" thinks Charlie, who sees her leaving out of the corner of her eye. Her arm muscles are burning. Frida's movements are becoming slower. They won't be able to hold out much longer.

"Stoooooooop!" the babboons' leader yells down from his perch on the rock. The troop immediately halt their attack. In disbelief, they all stare upward. Savage Claw is standing behind the leader, holding him in a headlock and pressing the tip of her dagger against his stomach. "Weapons down!" she yells, pressing the dagger a little harder against the leader's large belly.

He squeaks and frantically pats the ground with his palms. Immediately, the other baboons drop their spears. Savage Claw carefully steps backward, dragging her captive off the rock and toward the boat. "Back to the ship!" she shouts to Charlie and Frida. They run over and take up position on either side of her. Muriel flies down from her palm tree and takes up the rear. Surrounded by the raging and snarling baboons, they frogmarch the leader toward the boat. Whenever the baboons get too close, Savage Claw pokes the leader, making him squeak. Just a few more steps to the boat! They get in and Frida pushes the boat back into the water. They row back to the ***Anne Bonny*** *with their prisoner under close guard. On the beach, the baboons shriek with rage, beating their chests and leaping wildly into the air. Once back on the pirate ship, Savage Claw climbs up onto the bow* with the baboons' leader under her arm. With a mighty kick to his plump red behind, she sends him into the sea. Exhausted, the pirates collapse onto the deck and watch him swimming ashore, thrashing wildly in the water. "Let's get out of here!" groans Charlie, struggling back to her feet. Savage Claw extends a paw, Frida grabs it and lets the lynx help her up. Together they weigh anchor and hoist the sail.*

* Bow: the front of a ship.

For two days and two nights the pirates sail the sea until finally the Nightmare *appears on the horizon. It is drifting slowly with tattered sails. Tyra the Terrible has been sewing their remnants together. One of the rabid badgers, One Ear, is mending the hull with hammer, nail, and boards, while his brothers are arguing on deck.*

Savage Claw steps up to Charlie: "There's a lot to do," she mutters, reaching out her paw to shake Charlie's, "but I think we can handle it."

Charlie deftly steers the **Anne Bonny** *sideways toward the* Nightmare *so that Savage Claw can jump back onto her ship in one big leap. As the two pirate ships move away from each other, Charlie looks back once more. The lynx stands at the helm, raises a paw, and waves to her.*

Where Is Sakiba?

“Where is she?” thinks Charlie as she drums the ground with her hind legs. It’s Monday once again and she is waiting for Sakiba at the old oak tree. “Another hide-and-seek? Do I have to go look for her? Or did she forget me?”

Charlie sniffs, listens carefully, intently searching the bushes, the trees, and the meadow with her eyes.

“Something’s wrong.”

An uneasy feeling steals over her. Soon, she heads for Frida’s bear den and knocks on the door. “Sakiba wasn’t at the oak tree. It’s strange. I need to know what’s going on. Can you come with me?”

“This way,” Charlie says a bit later, squeezing between two bushes to enter the Lost Forest. Muriel, who has joined her friends, takes a step back. “Are you sure? What if we get lost?”

But Charlie resolutely walks on, closely followed by Frida. Muriel mutters, “This is a stupid idea, a very stupid idea it is,” but the three friends continue deeper into the Lost Forest. Charlie tries to remember the way to the wolf’s cave.

"It was already pretty dark when Sakiba took me home, but I think we passed by that big root," she reasons. Muriel huddles close to Frida, clutching her friend's shaggy fur with her wing.

Charlie marches on ahead. Their path leads them over fallen trees, past a swampy bog, through a narrow, sharp-edged crevice in a rocky outcrop. Frida has to pull in her belly and step sideways to fit through. Again and again, Muriel's waddling feet trip over gnarled roots sticking up from the ground.

"Muriel, watch out for the blackberry bushes!" Frida warns. "Or you'll end up with thorns in your webbed feet." Using a dead branch, Charlie pushes the bushes out of her way.

"This really is a totally stupid idea," Muriel whines and stumbles on.

"There! The cave!" Charlie exclaims, pointing through the trees to a large rock. "Sakiba! Sakiiibaaa!" she calls into the gloomy cave from the entrance. Only her echo responds.

"She's not there. Can we go home now? Can we go home now?" Muriel quacks and tugs at Charlie's foreleg.

But Charlie shakes her head. She turns on her wolf's eye and scans the surroundings.

Over there! Fresh tracks! Charlie bends over the prints.

"Maybe she went for a walk," Frida grumbles, and Muriel pleads: "I want to go home now! I want to go home, right now!"

But Charlie doesn't seem to hear her.

“These tracks are not Sakiba’s,” she says suddenly. Her heart races. “Look, one paw print is missing a toe. And the vegetable patch is all trampled!”

Without thinking, Charlie dashes into the cave, leaving her befuddled friends behind. “Sakiba!” she screams as she pushes deeper and deeper into the darkness.

Soon there is no longer enough light to distinguish the outlines of the cave . Charlie presses herself against the cool rock and feels her way forward with sweaty paws. Eventually, she sees a faint light flickering ahead. She heads toward it. The dancing light chases flitting shadows across the cave walls.

"Charlie!" she hears her friends calling from the cave entrance. What happened here? An overturned oil lamp lies on the floor, still burning. Charlie picks it up and turns up the flame. Chairs have been knocked over. A table is broken down the middle. Smashed crockery is scattered everywhere. Sakiba's storage jars with dried beetles and mealworms are broken. Her fishing rod is on the ground, snapped in two.

"There was a fight," flashes through Charlie's mind. With the oil lamp in her paw, she stumbles out of the wolf den to her friends. "They kidnapped Sakiba!" she stammers.

In her mind, she hears the voice of the wolf: "They'd kill me if they found me."

As fast as their legs can carry them, the three run from the forest. At the old oak tree, they separate to fetch their parents.

Panting, Charlie yanks open the door to the workshop. "Papa, you have to come right away! The wolf has been kidnapped!"

"Oh, Charlie, don't talk nonsense," Papa Rabbit replies, planing a table leg. But Charlie doesn't let up. She pesters her father until he finally hits the table leg with the plane and raises his voice.

"Darn it! Can't you see I'm working? Stop bothering me with your stories! It's not funny."

Charlie flinches, turns on her heel and storms into the rabbit house.

"Mama, you have to come right away! The wolf ...."

Mama Rabbit glares at her, telephone in paw: "Shh!" she hisses and covers the microphone with her paw. "My boss is on the line."

"But Mama! Sakiba has been kidnapped!"
repeats Charlie, tugging at her mother's stubby tail.
Her mother spins round and hisses "Charlie!
Not now!"
Angry and exasperated, Charlie stomps on the floor,
slams the front door, and runs back to the old oak tree.
Her two friends have fared no better. Muriel's
mother was busy with the little ones' swimming lessons.
"They were all quacking, splashing, and chattering all
over the place, and when I called out to Mama, she just
dove under water," Muriel says.
Frida's father was asleep on the sofa after a long shift in
the bakery and she had hardly been able to wake him.
"When I finally got him awake and told him everything,
he just said we weren't allowed in the Lost Forest, anyway,
and went right back to sleep!" Frida reports.
Nobody listens. Nobody has time.
"I'll have to find her myself," Charlie murmurs.
Muriel's eyes widen. She starts panting.
"Are you crazy?"
Frida puts her heavy paw on Charlie's shoulder.
"You can't go by yourself. I'm coming with you."
The duck shakes her head and stays behind,
quivering, as her friends set off.

For Charlie and Frida the plan is clear: return to the wolf's cave and pick up the trail from there!

They have only come a short distance when they are startled by crackling and rustling sounds behind them. Charlie wheels round and sees Muriel running after them. "Wait for me! Wait!" she quacks.

Soon, the three of them make their way through the Lost Forest. Muriel starts whistling to herself.

"Be quiet!" admonishes Charlie. But the duck doesn't stop. Charlie is getting impatient. "Shut up now! The wolves might hear us!"

Muriel flaps a wing in front of her beak and whispers: "But when you whistle, you're less afraid."

"You can climb on my back," Frida murmurs. Muriel flutters up and digs her wings into her bear friend's fur. Now they can walk faster, too, and they arrive at the wolf's cave in no time.

"They went this way!" Charlie says, pointing to the wolf track with the missing toe. She picks up the scent and sniffs the ground with her nose.

As they pass a boggy spot, the prints become deeper and more distinct. The friends stop and Charlie examines the tracks more closely.

"Here, drag marks. They're dragging Sakiba behind them. She's probably tied up. There's one track on the left and one on the right. And this one is a little bigger. There are at least four wolves!"

"F ... fo ... four?" stammers Muriel and buries her face in Frida's fur.

"Keep going," Charlie says confidently and they follow the paw prints.

It is already dark when the three friends arrive at a clearing. In the moonlight, they see the ruins of an abandoned castle. Its impressive main tower stretches high into the sky, reaching above the tallest trees. Most of the remaining walls have collapsed. Bits and pieces of brickwork are scattered among the rocks.

Suddenly, they hear the howl of a single wolf: "Ahhwooooo!" and immediately several others join in. Charlie feels a chill run down her spine. She stops in her tracks, as does Frida. Rooted to the spot, they stare at each other in fright. Muriel whimpers on Frida's back, her beak chattering.

"Be quiet. We'll sneak up on them," Charlie whispers to her friends, resolutely forcing her trembling legs forward, step by step by step.

Frida presses her belly to the ground and crawls after her. Muriel clamps a wing over her beak to stop the chattering and whistling. They creep alongside the crumbled wall until they come to a gap in the masonry.

The three of them press their heads together and peer through the gap. On the other side, a wide courtyard lies in darkness. At its center, a fire is ablaze, its flames leaping up high into the night sky. A little way from the fire a stake has been driven into the ground. Sakiba is tied to it, her head drooping! Five wolves prowl in a circle around her. They bare their teeth and growl. When the biggest wolf sits down, the others follows. The pack has surrounded Sakiba. They all listen to the leader.

"You thought you could escape," he growls at Sakiba. "No one escapes the pack! You betrayed us and for that you will die!"

Slowly, Sakiba raises her head and looks the leader straight in the eye. "Betray? Just because I didn't want to hunt?"

"You let the deer get away. On purpose! That was prey for all of us!" A scrawny, scarred wolf with a tooth-marked snout salivates. "Let me kill her!" he yelps to the leader, as strings of drool drip from his mouth.

"Silence!" the leader growls through clenched teeth, slapping the scar-faced wolf's jaw with his paw, causing another yelp.

The leader of the pack turns his head to Sakiba, his eyes full of hate. "Never before has a wolf dared to refuse the final test. *Hunt! Kill! Share the prey! That is the way of the wolf. Those who resist will die.*"

Sakiba spits on the ground in front of him. "I would rather die than follow you," she says in contempt. Her gaze pierces him.

Thoughts race around Charlie's head and she can feel her heartbeat all the way up her throat. "She must not die! What am I going to do? What would **Anne Bonny***do?"

Charlie closes her eyes and dives deep into her pirate world. In a fraction of a second, countless images and entire adventures race through her mind. Then like a flash of lightning, she knows what to do!

Charlie opens her eyes and whispers to her friends in a low, clear voice: "I'll distract the wolves. You untie Sakiba."

She jumps onto Frida's back and from there onto the wall. She scrambles along the top of the wall until she reaches the other side of the fire.

Below, the wolves close in on Sakiba, hissing through bared teeth, "Hunt, kill, share the prey. Hunt, kill, share the prey."

* **Anne Bonny** was one of the most famous female pirates of all time, and Charlie's pirate ship is named after her. **Anne Bonny** was born in Ireland in 1698. Women were not allowed on pirate ships at that time, so she disguised herself as a man at first. She later teamed up with another famous pirate named Mary Read. From then on, the two sailed across the Caribbean and were notorious and feared plunderers.

At that moment Charlie puts her paw in her mouth and blows a loud whistle. The wolves' heads spin round.

"Charlie, no! Get out of here!" screams Sakiba, writhing in her bonds.

"Prey," the scar-faced drooler yells as he catches sight of the rabbit girl.

Charlie puts her paws on her hips and stands up tall on the wall as the wolves move in closer. "You call yourselves a pack? A sorry pack you are! Let Sakiba go free! Every animal can choose its own way!" she shouts from the wall.

Now all five wolves are gathered at the foot of the wall, looking up at Charlie. One licks his muzzle and calls out, "Are you coming down, rabbit, or do you want us to come bag you?"

Charlie narrows her eyes to slits, "Get out of our forest! Sakiba belongs to *my* pack now."

Hearing this from the little rabbit girl standing on the wall with eyes flashing and paws planted on her hips, the wolves burst out laughing. They roll on the ground, holding their bellies with laughter.

"Sakiba in a rabbit pack. Hahahaha! That's a fate worse than death!" yowls a wolf with black fur and sickly yellow eyes.

"What's that duck doing over there?" the leader suddenly yelps. The others immediately turn their heads to follow his gaze. Muriel is frantically chafing Sakiba's ropes with a sharp-edged stone.

Sakiba twists around to her: "Save yourself!" she pleads.

But Muriel only chafes faster with her stone and begins to whistle loudly to counter her fear.

“Get that fowl!” the leader of the pack shouts. Immediately, the other wolves rush toward Muriel.

Muriel whistles even louder and higher, working faster.

Then Frida bursts through the bushes with a deafening roar and leaps toward the wolves, claws splayed and maw wide open. With a devastating swing of her paw, she hurls a black wolf against the wall. She picks up a second one by the scruff of the neck with her teeth and shakes him until he yelps and howls. The scar-faced wolf dashes towards Muriel, lunging at her wing. Just at that moment, Sakiba manages to tear the worn ropes and intercept him. The two wolves roll on the ground, snarling and snapping at each other. The leader and another wolf are coming at Frida from two sides, cornering her. Frida backs away, her teeth still buried in the third wolf’s neck.

Up on the wall, Charlie realizes what the two wolves intend. They’re going to jump at her friend from the left and the right at the same time. Now even the black wolf Frida hurled against the wall gets up again and shakes his head in a daze. She has to act! Bold as a pirate, she jumps from the high wall, breaking her fall by rolling onto the soft grass.

She dashes over to the fire and grabs a large branch sticking out at the side. She holds the burning branch in front of her like a torch, sneaking up on the leader from behind.

When his tail catches fire, he howls in fright, leaps up, and darts away into the night.

Frida takes advantage of the confusion and swings the wolf in her mouth at the enemy to her right.

Sakiba now stands over scar-face and presses her teeth threateningly against his throat. Caught off guard, outmatched and robbed of their leader, the wolves tuck in their tails and race away.

“Ha! Take that!” cries Charlie, raising the torch in the air.

Muriel prances around boxing her wings and shouts, “We gave it to them! We gave it to them!”

“That was close,” Frida snorts and puts her paw on Charlie’s back.

Together they set off toward home. While the three friends talk excitedly about what just happened, Sakiba silently trots along beside them. When the three quiet down, she says, “You put yourselves in great danger. You shouldn’t have done that.”

Charlie nudges the wolf in the side. “In our pack, we take care of each other.”

“Yes. And you don’t know how proud I am to belong to this pack,” Sakiba replies.

As they approach the edge of the Lost Forest, they hear voices calling to them from afar, “Charlie! Frida! Muriel! Where are you?!”

“Here!” shouts Muriel as she runs toward the clearing.

Charlie and Frida follow her, only the wolf lags behind.

The whole village community has set out with torches to look for the three friends. Mrs. Lynx is the first to spot the three girls through the trees. "There they are!" she shouts.
Everyone rushes over, and the parents hug their children.
"What were you thinking, going into the Lost Forest at night all alone? You could have been hurt!" Mama Rabbit says, embracing her daughter.
Mama Duck strokes Muriel's head with her wing: "We were so worried!"
The trio of friends start telling everyone what happened in the forest. "We had to help the wolf," Charlie explains.
At this, her father looks at her sternly and shakes his head. "Charlie! Now stop telling these made-up wolf stories!"
"She's telling the truth," comes a voice from the forest.
Sakiba steps through the bushes into the open. "And if it weren't for Charlie and her friends, I wouldn't have survived this night."
Her words are followed by a hushed silence. Astonished, the adults listen to Sakiba's account of the night.
When Papa Bear learns what danger his daughter put herself in, he has to steady himself on the old oak tree: "Frida! Why didn't you come and get us?"
Mama Rabbit and Mrs. Duck nod in agreement.
"We tried to!" says Charlie, "But you're always so busy, and then you don't listen at all!"

The Performance

“Charlie! Hurry up!” says Mama Rabbit. Then she winks at her daughter. “Come on, I’ll help you.”

She zips up the zipper on the back of Charlie’s dress with a flourish. “You look great.”

Charlie examines her blue dress with butterflies in the mirror from all sides.

“Are you coming?” Papa Rabbit calls from the hallway.

Charlie races down the stairs, Mama Rabbit hurrying after her.

As Mama Rabbit straightens Papa Rabbit’s tie, she tilts her head back in surprise. “Herbert! Did you wear your good shirt and coat in the workshop?”

“You’re all sawdusty,” Charlie giggles, brushing off her father’s shirt and coat.

He squirms in his suit and grumbles. “This is so uncomfortable. I can hardly move!”

“It’s just for tonight, Herbert. I think you look very handsome,” Mama Rabbit says, pressing a kiss to her husband’s cheek.

Charlie hops ahead to the old oak tree, whistling. When she gets there, she can hardly keep herself from laughing out loud: Sakiba waits by the tree, motionless and majestic like a statue, while Muriel and her mother waddle round and round, quacking and flapping excitedly.

"Hurry! We have to go! Else we'll be late!" babbles Muriel, while her mother finally stops and nods her head vigorously.

Charlie looks at Muriel. She looks very pretty with a big blue bow on her head.

"Looks great on you, that bow," she says.

Muriel is pleased. "It's new. I made it myself. All by myself. If you want, I'll make one for you. And for you too, Sakiba."

"Uh, thanks," Sakiba replies, looking a little lost. "But now we really do have to go."

The group starts off toward the school. Muriel and Charlie rush ahead because they want to get the best seats. Charlie's parents chat with Sakiba while Mrs. Duck urges everyone to hurry.

Today is the day before summer vacation! The school has built a stage on the soccer field just for the end-of-year show. The performance will be *Swan Lake*!

Before long, Charlie is sitting next to Muriel and her parents on the bleachers. Slowly, the heavy, dark red curtain rises, revealing a magnificent stage set: a lake glistening in the moonlight, surrounded by mighty trees. The outlines of a regal castle can be seen through rising clouds of mist.

The audience is breathless: Papa and Mama Bear, Sakiba, Charlie's parents, Mrs. Lynx, and the whole village community watch the performance open mouthed. "Ohs" and "Ahs" ripple across the bleachers. Mama Rabbit wraps her arm around her daughter and presses Charlie's head against her cheek.
The music plays and Frida dances onto the stage, followed by the three white swans. With flowing, elegant movements, the bear throws the swans high into the air. With half-stretched wings, they slowly glide back down to the ground and turn pirouettes.

Muriel wipes a tear from the corner of her eye.
"Beautiful! So beautiful! Frida dances even more beautifully than before," she whispers to Charlie.
Charlie thinks about how Frida mustered courage after her adventure in the forest. She told Mrs. Peacock, the ballet teacher, that she wanted to dance in the performance. When Mrs. Peacock refused, the three little swans stood by the bear and said, "then we won't dance either! It's all of us or none!"
Charlie smiles to herself. Since Sakiba's rescue, a lot has changed. Every Monday, Charlie meets with the wolf to be instructed further in all the arts of the wolf's eye. Increasingly, and with greater ease, she succeeds in being fully present at school, listening, and participating. She has improved enough for a "satisfactory" grade or two and a "*Keep it up!*" stamp from Mrs. Lynx. And when she drifts off into a dream, Muriel usually gives her a nudge and reminds her of her task. Like now.
"Charlie, the performance!" whispers her friend, leaning into her.
As the curtain falls, the whole village shouts and applauds from the bleachers. All the animals in Frida's class send up a great cheer with paws, hooves, and webbed feet, shouting "Frida! Frida!"
Sakiba, sitting next to Frida's parents, stretches up her snout and howls a long-drawn-out "Ahhwoooooo!" into the night.

On stage, Frida and the swans take one deep bow after another. The applause goes on and on. When the dancers finally descend the small staircase, Charlie and Muriel rush to the front.

"You were great!" they shout and hug Frida.

One by one, the adults also arrive and congratulate the dancers.

"Actually quite superb," Mrs. Lynx purrs, offering her paw in congratulation. "A wonderful piece! The staging, the harmony between you dancers: grand! And the beautiful stage design! It impressed me very much."

Frida grabs hold of Charlie, who is talking to Sakiba, and pulls her over. "Charlie painted that."

Astonished, Mrs. Lynx turns to Charlie: "Wow, Charlie! I didn't know you were an artist! How did you do that?"

"Rabbit's eye," Sakiba whispers from the side and winks at Charlie.

The End

Charlie's Bag of Tricks

On the following pages, Charlie introduces you to her collection of tips and tricks, including her other wolf training lessons.

Some printable materials are also available that a grown-up can help you access. If you would like the materials, please show the following instructions to an adult:

Notes on Supplementary Materials
The following materials that complement this book can be downloaded free of charge once you register on the Hogrefe website:

1. The wolf's eye is valuable when.../daydreaming is valuable when... poster
2. Using the wolf's eye at school and while studying poster
3. Strengths sheet
4. Cutout figure of Sakiba

How to proceed:

1. Go to www.hgf.io/media and create a user account. If you already have one, please log in.
2. Go to **My supplementary materials** in your account dashboard and enter the code below. You will automatically be redirected to the download area, where you can access and download the supplementary materials.

Code: B-W4MPIG

To make sure you have permanent direct access to all the materials, we recommend that you download them and save them on your device.

Uncle Louis' When–Then Plan

A "when–then plan" helps you to:

- remember something important when you need to; and
- follow through on your plan of action for a certain situation.

Here's how it works: Say to yourself, "When X happens, then I do Y right away."
For example:

- "When the teacher announces a test, then I take out my homework notebook and write down the date right away."
- "When I finish my homework, then I put it in my school bag for the next day right away."
- "When I walk out of the locker room, then I look back right away to make sure I haven't left anything lying around or on a hook."

To make sure your when–then plan works well, you'll need to train yourself to use it. Draw it on a poster or write it down in a notebook. Then make yourself comfortable, lying down on your bed or on the floor. If you like, you can close your eyes.

Homework

Imagine the situation in your plan exactly. Here's an example: "Well ... it's Tuesday after gym class. I change my clothes and go to the door. I say to myself, '*When I walk out of the locker room, then I look back right away to make sure I haven't left anything lying around or on a hook.*'" You can also say the phrase out loud. Imagine a picture or movie of how you look back to the locker room at that moment and discover, for example, that your jacket is still hanging on a hook or your gym shorts are still on the floor. In your mind, go back and pick up the item. Maybe you are even a little proud of yourself and glad that you didn't forget anything.

And now it's your turn. What do you want to achieve? What do you want to remember to do in the future? In which situation would you like to react differently? Write it down:

When ____

____

Then, right away, I _________________________________

____

Practice only *one* when–then plan at a time. As soon as you always remember to follow the plan without having to think about it, you can make a new plan for something else.

Your parents and teachers can help you by:

- creating a nice poster with you, maybe even with photos, like Charlie and Uncle Louis did;
- practicing the plan with you in an imaginary journey or even playacting with you;
- reminding you of the plan; and
- giving you a compliment when you carry out the plan.

Papa Rabbit's Clean-Up Strategy

Do you hate cleaning up as much as Charlie does? Do you sometimes not know where to put all your stuff? Do you just stand around in your room and look at the chaos as if paralyzed? Do you often misplace things? Then find ways to keep things simple!

- Extremely neat people know exactly where everything belongs and may have rules like: "Everything has its place! Books are sorted on the shelf by size or color; toys go back into their original boxes." This makes everything look very pretty, but it can be tiresome. For regular bunnies, it is enough if everything looks just reasonably neat: throw all the toys in a big box and slide it under the bed.

- Make sure you have a laundry basket in the room that you can use as a basketball hoop. Can you make the perfect shot from the bed with your dirty socks, panties, and t-shirts?

- Ask your parents to help you cover your schoolbooks in different colors and use differently colored folders. Pick a matching color for each subject: maybe blue for math and yellow for English – or the other way round?
  This way you can quickly find the right folders and books when unpacking and don't have to read the covers.

- Designate a "school bag parking space" and get into the habit of always putting your school bag there. In the beginning, a when–then plan can help you remember to use it: "*When I get home, then I put my school bag in its parking space right away.*"

Homework Tricks for Bunnies

Charlie figured out how to concentrate better when studying and doing homework with a little help from her mother and Mrs. Lynx. She uses the following tricks:

1. Make a plan. What task do you want to start with? What do you want to accomplish in the next 10 to 15 minutes?
2. Get out all the materials you will need for the task (folders, worksheets, pencil, books).
3. Set the alarm clock for 10 or 15 minutes.
4. Think to yourself, "What is my task?" Repeat in your own words what you have to do.
5. Say to yourself "Wolf's eye on: go!" and dive into the task.
6. Take a short break (3–5 minutes) when the alarm goes off.

It's good to take a break before you feel tired. Then it is easier for you to start studying again.
During your break, you can listen to music, walk around a bit, eat or drink a little, do a wolf's eye exercise, or look out the window.

Don't let yourself get totally absorbed by something new. If you watch a video, read comics, start building something with Lego, or start playing a game during your break, you'll find it very hard to stop.

Charlie took far too long to do her homework at first. She had almost no free time left. That's not good! If you feel the same way, then talk to your parents and your teacher, and ask them if you can stop after a specific amount of time.

Daydreaming Is Valuable

Sakiba says:

*"Daydreaming is valuable, at the right time.
And the wolf's eye is valuable, at the right time."*

Charlie thought about this with her friends and designed a poster.
What do you think? When and how do daydreaming and your imagination help you? What would you like to use the wolf's eye for?

Wolf's Eye

When I have the wolf's eye, I am at one with the task. I focus on the task with all my senses and I am fully absorbed. I don't let myself be distracted by anything or anyone.

This is valuable when:

... I study, do homework, take a test, or complete a task.

... I have to listen.

... I clean up or work on some difficult problem.

... I have to do several things in a row without forgetting anything (e.g., when I have to get dressed, eat breakfast, and brush my teeth in the morning and don't have much time; when I want to take home from school everything I need for homework; or when I make my weekly schedule at school).

Daydreaming

When I daydream, I let my thoughts wander. I detach myself from the here and now and dive into my imagination.

This is valuable when:

... I am stuck on a problem and need new ideas.

... I have lots of time and want to relax.

... I want to do something creative, for example, draw something or write a story.

... I want to keep myself from forgetting something by picturing it in my mind exactly, like in a photograph or a movie.

... I want to imagine something that has not yet happened or that does not yet exist.

The Wolf's Eye

Dreaming and using your imagination: Charlie is a master of this.
After her encounter with Sakiba, Charlie is determined to learn the wolf's eye, which all wolves practice for years. Sakiba says:

"First, a wolf must be fully present.
Then she needs to sharpen her senses."

Here, Sakiba and Charlie will let you in on some secret wolf training exercises. You already know a few of them.

Wolf Exercise 1: Follow Your Breathing

Lie on your back with your legs and arms stretched out on the floor so you can relax comfortably.
If you want, you can close your eyes. Or you may prefer to look at a point on the ceiling (where your gaze can come to rest).
Pay attention to how your head feels as it rests on the floor. Notice how your shoulders are touching the floor ... your upper back ... your arms ... your hands ... your legs ... and your feet. Now let your attention move onto your breathing. Notice how it feels to breathe in and out.

Your breaths come and go all by themselves ... without effort ... at their own pace – there is no right or wrong way to breathe.
Now notice exactly how you inhale. When do you start breathing in? Follow the air flowing into your body until the very last moment ... In ... In ... In ... In ... In ...
Now pay attention to how you exhale. Can you feel the moment when the air begins to flow out of you? Can you follow the exhalation to the very last moment, until it is completely over? Out ... Out ... Out ... Out ... Out ...
Stay with your breathing and follow it.
Now pay attention to each breath, the breathing in and the breathing out. In ... out ... in ... out ... in ... out ... Where do you feel your breath most? Where does it move your body?
Stay in this moment a little while just by yourself. When you're ready, you can open your eyes and sit up slowly.
How do you feel?

You can also do this exercise sitting down, just like Charlie did on her rock. Sit upright but relaxed like a king or queen on a throne. You can rest your hands comfortably on your thighs or knees.

Wolf Exercise 2: The Chestnut Leaf

One day in autumn Charlie was late for wolf training. All the way to Sakiba's cave, she kept stopping to look at the beautifully colored autumn leaves and to gather chestnuts! Sakiba smiled to herself and said, "You just gave me an idea, Charlie. Today I'll show you a very special wolf training exercise."

Choose a hand to be your "chestnut leaf." Stretch out all your fingers with the palm facing toward you so your hand looks like a chestnut leaf. Make sure you have some space between your fingers. Now, use the index finger of your other hand to trace around the outer edge of your "chestnut leaf," starting at your wrist (at the base of your little finger).

If you wish, you can now close your eyes. Concentrate on exactly how it feels as your index finger goes around your chestnut leaf hand.

Slowly move your index finger along the outer edge of your little finger, up ... and back down the other side.

Pay close attention to how it feels. Trace each finger one at a time, up ... and down the other side ... until you reach the other side of your hand.

Now direct your attention to your breath. Breathe in calmly, slowly running your index finger back along the chestnut leaf hand. Have you reached the top of the thumb? Then exhale while tracing down. Outline each finger in this way – inhale and trace up, exhale and trace down – until you reach the other side of your hand. Breathe normally and let each breath set the pace for your finger to follow. If thoughts enter your mind, that's ok. Just let them blow by like leaves in the wind and turn your attention back to your breathing.

Repeat a few times and notice how your breath and your index finger connect to one another.

Now open your eyes and you're wide awake!

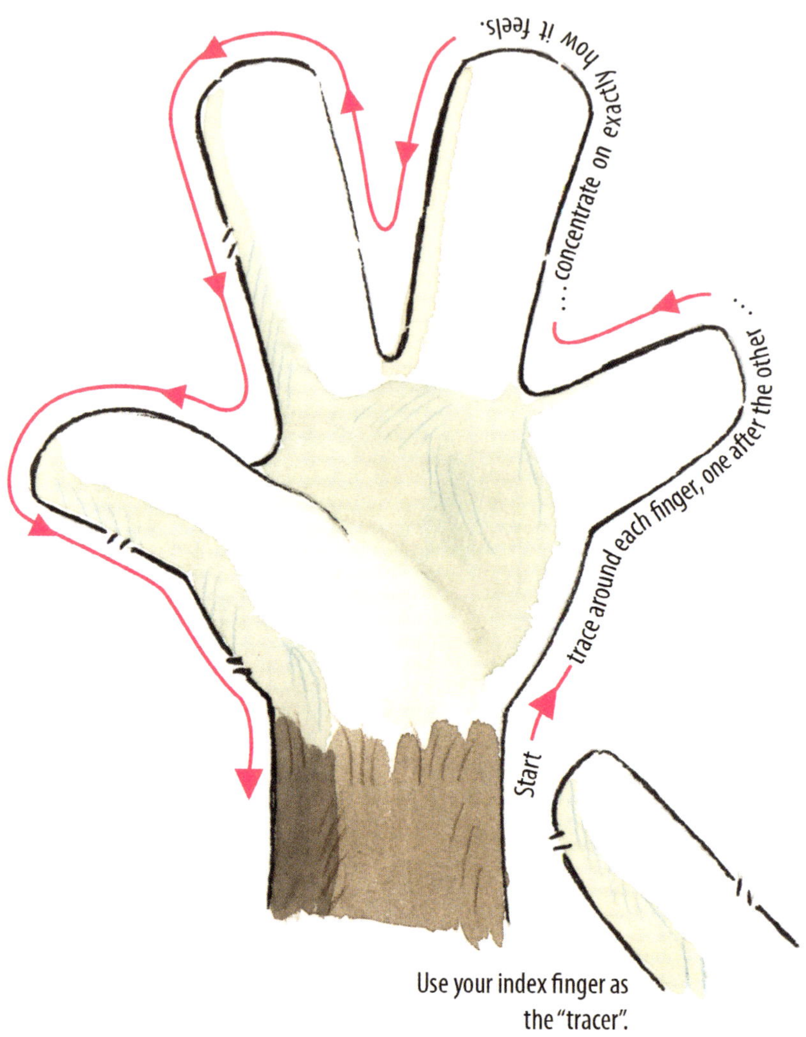

Start
trace around each finger, one after the other . . .
. . . concentrate on exactly how it feels.
Use your index finger as the "tracer".

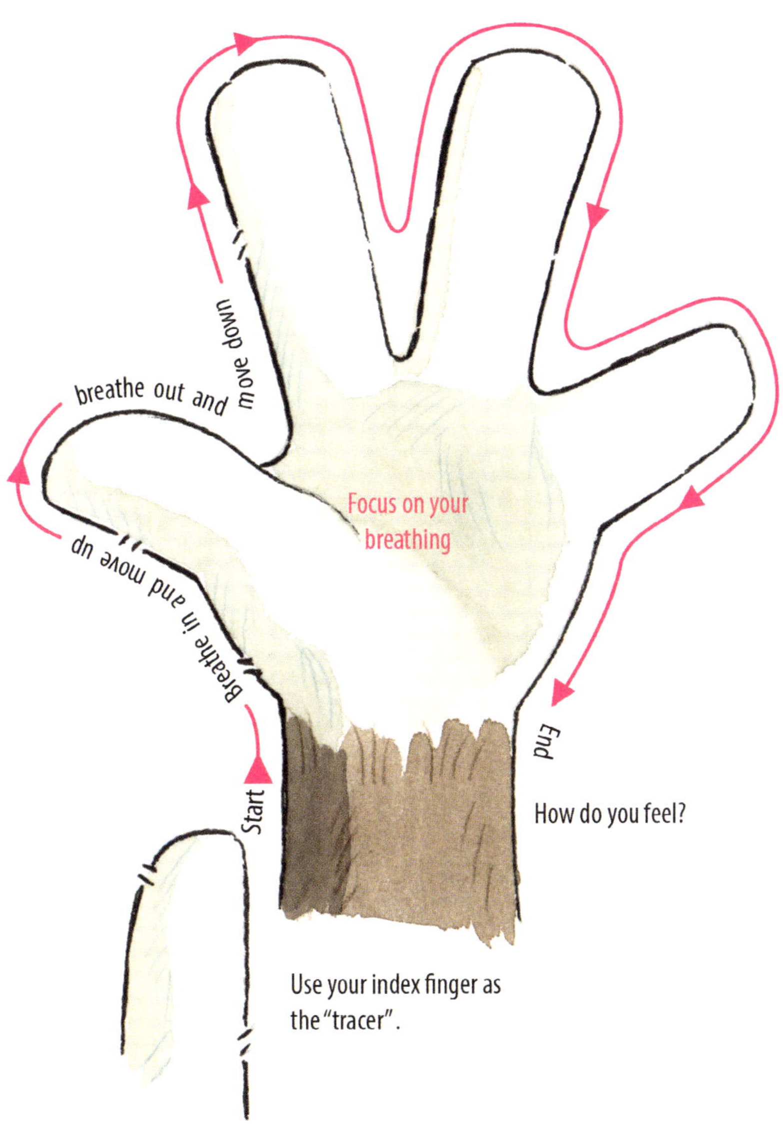
Start
Breathe in and move up
breathe out and move down
Focus on your breathing
End
How do you feel?
Use your index finger as the "tracer".

Wolf Exercise 3: What Do I See, Hear, Feel?

You already know this exercise.

Sit on a chair in a comfortable position, perhaps placing both feet on the floor. Put your hands comfortably on your thighs. And now just concentrate on what you see, taking your time.
Now, close your eyes or just look down, whichever you prefer.
Concentrate on what you hear ... on all the sounds around you ....
If you like, take notice of your body: How do your feet feel on the floor? Where exactly do you feel the chair you are sitting on? How do your hands feel? Your shoulders?
Now pay attention to your breathing. Where does the breath move your body? How does it feel to breathe in? How does it feel to breathe out? Where can you feel the breath in your body?
If you notice that you are getting lost in thoughts, turn your attention to the thoughts ... and then back again to your breath.
Continue like this for a little while. When you are ready, you can slowly come back ...
Rub your hands together and you're wide awake!

Wolf Exercise 4: Charlie's Journey Into a Wolf's Body

When Charlie found Sakiba in the Lost Forest, tied to a stake and threatened by her old pack, she had to act fast. She used her imagination, diving deep into her pirate world, to figure out what the pirate Anne Bonny would do. This is how she mustered the courage and forged the plan to fend off the pack of wolves.

Since then, Charlie uses her imagination often to learn from other people and adopt their skills and good qualities. She puts herself in someone else's shoes and imagines exactly how they move, think, feel, and act.

To sharpen the wolf's eye even further, Charlie imagines being Sakiba. This is how she does it:*

Charlie sits on a rock in front of the rabbit house and looks with pride at the picture of Sakiba she has drawn. She drew the wolf striding through the forest, alert, focused, and with sharpened senses and a springy stride. Charlie studies the drawing and commits all its details to memory. She closes her eyes.

She feels the light wind in her fur and the sun warming her back.

* It can be hard to imagine being a wolf at the beginning. It works better if you have the text read aloud to you two or three times. As soon as you have become more familiar with the text, you can concentrate better on your own inner images and feelings.

She straightens her back, holds up her head, and flexes her shoulders – like a wolf. She takes a few deep breaths and calls up the image of Sakiba in her mind's eye.

As she slowly breathes in and out, she imagines the wolf roaming the forest. “Alert, focused, with sharpened senses,” Charlie whispers. With each breath, the inner image becomes clearer.

In her imagination, Charlie feels what it is like to slip into a wolf’s body, and continues striding through the forest.

Can you do it too? Can you slip away from your body into Sakiba’s? Your hands and feet turn into wolf paws.

Can you feel the forest floor beneath you with your paws?

How does it feel to be a wolf? Feel your muscles: powerful and supple.

You stride through the forest. Your wolf’s eye is fixed on the path, taking in everything so you can move quickly and surely toward your goal.

You dash past trees and bushes. Light-footed, you jump over obstacles, see every root and rock. You are awake, focused, completely a wolf.

Through your wolf’s nose the fresh forest air flows deep into your body, calm and steady. A wolf can run like this for hours and still feel light and strong. Your wolf’s ears are sharp: you hear everything more distinctly. Can you hear the sounds of the forest? Gusts of wind, the rustling of leaves, the muffled sound of your steps?

With every step, every breath, you can absorb more of Sakiba: to concentrate, to be alert, and to better focus your attention whenever you need to.

Know this: whenever you want to concentrate – for school, studying, or sports – you can call up the Sakiba in you. It may help to think: "Look closely, listen carefully – alert as the wolf."

You can take some time to wander through the woods as Sakiba, then come back to your own body, slowly, at your own pace.

What was it like for you to be Sakiba? What did you visualize specifically? Was there anything that bothered you? What could you change in the story so that you could better slip into the wolf inside you?

Using the Wolf's Eye at School and While Studying

When Charlie does homework or tries to concentrate at school, she uses the wolf's eye and makes use of this lesson from Sakiba:

"Wolves stay focused on their task and never lose sight of their goal."

1. I ask myself, "What is my task?"
   - I read the assignment carefully (or listen carefully when someone explains what I have to do).
   - I repeat in my own words what I have to do (out loud or in my mind).

2. I say to myself, "Wolf's eye on! Go!" and dive into the task.

3. With each breath, I gather all my attention and focus it on the task.

When I'm done, I move on to step four:

4. After completing each task, I check: "Did I finish everything? Is the answer correct?"
   - If I made a mistake or forgot something: Good! I caught it!
   - I correct it immediately.

5. I work on one task at a time, one after the other, and never lose sight of my goal.

6. When I finish, I am proud that I focused like a wolf – ahhwooooo!

Frida's and Muriel's Strengths Poster

For a long time, Charlie has the feeling that everyone can see only her weaknesses and constantly criticizes her. In her essay, she even writes that she can't do anything well except draw, and that drawing doesn't count at school. Luckily, Muriel and Frida make her a strengths poster on page 130. Maybe you'd like to become a personal strengths detective , too? Here's how:

- First, think about your own strengths:
  - What are you particularly good at? What comes easily to you?
  - What are you interested in and what do you like to do?
  - What do you know a lot about?
  - What characteristics distinguish you? Are you helpful, kind, generous, brave, imaginative, funny, strong, or a good friend? Do you take good care of your pet, do you fight for what's right ...?
  - What compliments have you heard about yourself?
  - In which moments were you most proud of yourself?
  - What difficulties have you overcome? How did you manage that?

Sometimes we don't see our own strengths. Charlie only realizes that daydreaming is one of her strengths when Sakiba points it out. Maybe you have a hidden strength, too.

Find out!

Copy the strengths sheet shown on the next page and hand it out to two to five people you like (see page 198 for instructions on how to download a printable version of the strengths sheet). Prepare to be surprised by what your mother, father, grandfather, grandmother, aunts, uncles, neighbors, friends, or coaches write about you.

Dear ______________________________,

Can you help me find my strengths?

Please complete the following sentences and return the page to ______________________________

I am glad to know you because ...

I especially like this about you: ...

You can do this well: ...

I first noticed this when ...

Charlie's Pirate ABC

Anne Bonny: was born in Ireland in 1698. Women were not allowed on pirate ships at that time, so she disguised herself as a man at first. She later teamed up with another famous pirate named Mary Read. From then on, the two sailed across the Caribbean and were notorious and feared plunderers.

Berth: a shelf-like sleeping space on a ship.

Bow: the front of a ship.

Cabin: room in a ship where you live and sleep.

Caravel: a sailing ship with two to four masts.

Dinghy: a small rowboat carried on a bigger ship.

Hanging the jib: pirate slang for pouting or frowning.

Hatch: opening on a ship that can be closed with a board on hinges.

Helm: the steering wheel of a ship

Hoist the jib: raise the triangular foresail of a ship.

Landlubber: derogatory word for a person who is not used to going to sea.

Powder keg: a barrel of gunpowder.

Starboard: the right side of the ship as you're standing on it facing forward.

Stern: the rear of a ship.

The Science Background for Adults

Through the course of the story, Charlie the rabbit girl is initiated into "wolf training" by her mentor Sakiba. Part of the training is based on the technique of mindfulness-based stress reduction. For Jon Kabat-Zinn (1990), who is the best-known expert on mindfulness today, it involves an act of non-judgmental, intentional concentration and conscious direction of the mind onto the experience of the here and now. The wolf Sakiba integrates specific exercises for "focused attention or concentrative meditation" (for example, see Lippelt et al., 2014, or Ainsworth et al., 2013) into her wolf training. The instructions for these are adapted from Brunsting et al. (2013), Jensen et al. (2019), Kabat-Zinn (1990), Kaiser Greenland (2016), and Kaltwasser (2013, 2016; see also Kaltwasser et al., 2014). Sakiba's "chestnut leaf exercise" is taught by many mindfulness trainers, each in a slightly modified form, and is known as "take five," "five finger breathing," or "five finger meditation" (e.g., Bell, 2011; Children's Hospital of Wisconsin, 2020). Despite our extensive research, it remains unclear who originally developed this idea.

Several studies have shown that mindfulness practice has a positive effect on attentional performance and cognitive abilities as well as children's mental health and sense of well-being. For an overview, see Carsley et al., 2018, Linderkamp, 2020, and Zenner et al., 2014.

Charlie's "journey into a wolf's body" utilizes children's imagination. Children are often very good at empathizing with the roles of others and calling up images in their minds. That children can also use characteristics and skills of fictional characters in real life through role-playing or listening to stories has been shown by a number of studies (Haimovitz et al., 2019; Lee et al., 2014; Veraksa et al., 2019; White et al., 2017).

Since the 1970s, the training of children with learning or attention difficulties has also focused on teaching them how to use questions and internal instructions (self-instructions) to structure, prioritize, and consciously manage their attention and work behavior (e.g., Meichenbaum & Goodman, 1971). Sakiba's lesson, "wolves stay focused on their task and never lose sight of their goal," is based on this. "If–then plans" (or "when–then plans," as they are called here) are a specific form of self-instruction. They are particularly effective for translating intention into action. Uncle Louis shows Charlie how she can use them to reduce forgetfulness. The method was developed by the social and motivational psychologist Peter M. Gollwitzer (1999). Several studies have shown that children who have difficulty concentrating especially benefit from this method (for a good overview see Gawrilow, 2011).

Further Reading

Achtziger, A., Gollwitzer, P.M., & Sheeran, P. (2008). Implementation intentions and shielding goal striving from unwanted thoughts and feelings. *Personality and Social Psychology Bulletin, 34*, 381–393.

Adam, H., & Galinsky, A.D. (2012). Enclothed cognition. *Journal of Experimental Social Psychology, 48*(4), 918–925.

Ainsworth, B., Eddershaw, R., Meron, D., Baldwin, D.S., & Garner, M. (2013). The effect of focused attention and open monitoring meditation on attention network function in healthy volunteers. *Psychiatry Research, 210*(3), 1226–1231.

Belfi, A.M., Vessel, E.A., Brielmann, A., Isik, A.I., Chatterjee, A., Leder, H., Pelli, D.G., & Starr, G.G. (2019). Dynamics of aesthetic experience are reflected in the default-mode network. *Neuroimage, 188*, 584–597.

Bell, M. (2011). Five finger meditation. In T. Nhat Hanh, *Planting seeds: Practicing mindfulness with children* (pp. 87–88). Parallax Press.

Berman, M.G., Jonides, J., & Kaplan, S. (2008). The cognitive benefits of interacting with nature. *Psychological Science, 19*(12), 1207–1212.

Bozhilova, N.S., Michelini, G., Kuntsi, J., & Asherson, P. (2018). Mind wandering perspective on attention-deficit/hyperactivity disorder. *Neuroscience & Biobehavioral Reviews, 92*, 464–476.

Brunsting, M. , Nakamura, Y., & Simma, C. (2013). Wach und präsent – Achtsamkeit in Schule und Therapie [Awake and present: Mindfulness in schools and in therapy]. Haupt Verlag.

Carsley, D., Khoury, B., & Heath, N.L. (2018). Effectiveness of mindfulness interventions for mental health in schools: A comprehensive meta-analysis. *Mindfulness, 9*(3), 693–707.

Children's Wisconsin (2020). *Take 5ive*. https://www.healthykidslearnmore.com/Healthy-Kids-Learn-More/Educator-Resources/Take-5ive/Focus-and-Attention-K4-8

Cordingly, D. (2008, January 03). Bonny, Anne (1698–1782), pirate. In *Oxford dictionary of national biography*. https://www.oxforddnb.com/view/10.1093/ref:odnb/9780198614128.001.0001/odnb-9780198614128-e-39085

Franklin, M.S., Mrazek, M.D., Anderson, C.L., Johnston, C., Smallwood, J., Kingstone, A., & Schooler, J.W. (2017). Tracking distraction: The relationship between mind-wandering, meta-awareness, and ADHD symptomatology. *Journal of Attention Disorders, 21*(6), 475–486.

Gawrilow, C. (2011). Self-regulation in children with ADHD: How if–then plans improve executive functions and delay of gratification in children with ADHD. *The ADHD Report, 19*(6), 4.

Goleman, D. (2014). *Focus: The hidden driver of excellence*. Bloomsbury Paperbacks.

Gollwitzer, P.M. (1999). Implementation intentions: Strong effects of simple plans. *American Psychologist, 54*, 493–503.

Gollwitzer, P.M., & Sheeran, P. (2006). Implementation intentions and goal achievement: A meta-analysis of effects and processes. *Advances in Experimental Social Psychology, 38*, 69–119.

Haimovitz, K., Dweck, C.S., & Walton, G.M. (2019). Preschoolers find ways to resist temptation after learning that willpower can be energizing. *Developmental Science*, e12905.

Hasenkamp, W., Wilson-Mendenhall, C.D., Duncan, E., & Barsalou, L.W. (2012). Mind wandering and attention during focused meditation: a fine-grained temporal analysis of fluctuating cognitive states. *Neuroimage, 59*(1), 750–760.

Hölzel, B.K., Ott, U., Hempel, H., Hackl, A., Wolf, K., Stark, R., & Vaitl, D. (2007). Differential engagement of anterior cingulate and adjacent medial frontal cortex in adept meditators and non-meditators. *Neuroscience Letters, 421*(1), 16–21.

Jensen, H., Gøtzsche, K., Weppenaar Pedersen, C., & Sælebakke, A. (2019). *Hellwach und ganz bei sich: Achtsamkeit und Empathie in der Schule* [Wide awake and at one with yourself: Mindfulness and empathy in schools]. Beltz.

Kabat-Zinn, J. (1990). *Full catastrophe living: How to cope with stress, pain and illness using mindfulness meditation*. Dell.

Kaiser Greenland, S. (2016). *Mindful games: Sharing mindfulness and meditation with children, teens, and families*. Shambhala.

Kaltwasser, V. (2013). *Achtsamkeit in der Schule: Stille-Inseln im Unterricht: Entspannung und Konzentration* [Mindfulness in school contexts: Islands of stillness in the classroom: Relaxation and concentration]. Beltz.

Kaltwasser, V. (2016). *Praxisbuch Achtsamkeit in der Schule: Selbstregulation und Erziehungsfähigkeit als Basis von Bildung* [Handbook of mindfulness in schools: Self-regulation as the basis for education]. *Beltz*.

Kaltwasser, V., Sauer, S., & Kohls, N. (2014). Mindfulness in German Schools (MISCHO): A specifically tailored training program: Concept, implementation, and empirical results. In S. Schmidt & H. Walach (Eds.), *Meditation: Neuroscientific approaches and philosophical implications* (pp. 381–404). Springer International Publishing.

Kane, M.J., Brown, L.H., McVay, J.C., Silvia, P.J., Myin-Germeys, I., & Kwapil, T.R. (2007). For whom the mind wanders, and when: An experience-sampling study of working memory and executive control in daily life. *Psychological Science, 18*(7), 614–621.

Kaplan, S. (1995). The restorative benefits of nature: Toward an integrative framework. *Journal of Environmental Psychology, 15*(3), 169–182.

Kutscher, M.L., & Moran, M. (2009). *Organizing the disorganized child*. William Morrow Paperbacks.

Lee, K., Talwar, V., McCarthy, A., Ross, I., Evans, A., & Arruda, C. (2014). Can classic moral stories promote honesty in children? *Psychological Science, 25*(8), 1630–1636.

Linderkamp, F. (2020). The effectiveness of mindfulness based interventions with children and adolescents with ADHD: A systematic review. *Lernen und Lernstörungen, 9*(1), 25–35.

Lippelt, D.P., Hommel, B., & Colzato, L.S. (2014). Focused attention, open monitoring and loving kindness meditation: Effects on attention, conflict monitoring, and creativity: A review. *Frontiers in Psychology, 5*, 1083.

Meichenbaum, D.h., & Goodman, J. (1971). Training impulsive children to talk to themselves: A means of developing self-control. *Journal of Abnormal Psychology, 77*(2), 115–126. https://doi.org/10.1037/h0030773.

Miller-Wilson, K. *Pirate glossary*. https://reference.yourdictionary.com/resources/pirate-terms-phrases.html

Modesto-Lowe, V., Farahmand, P., Chaplin, M., & Sarro, L. (2015). Does mindfulness meditation improve attention in attention deficit hyperactivity disorder? *World Journal of Psychiatry, 5*(4), 397.

Mooneyham, B.W., & Schooler, J.W. (2013). The costs and benefits of mind-wandering: A review. *Canadian Journal of Experimental Psychology/Revue canadienne de psychologie expérimentale, 67*(1), 11.

Pallardy, R. (2019, November 28). Anne Bonny. In *Encyclopaedia Britannica*. https://www.britannica.com/biography/Anne-Bonny

Seli, P., Risko, E.F., & Smilek, D. (2016). On the necessity of distinguishing between unintentional and intentional mind wandering. *Psychological Science, 27*(5), 685–691.

Seli, P., Risko, E.F., Smilek, D., & Schacter, D.L. (2016). Mind-wandering with and without intention. *Trends in Cognitive Sciences, 20*(8), 605–617.

Seli, P., Smallwood, J., Cheyne, J.A., & Smilek, D. (2015). On the relation of mind wandering and ADHD symptomatology. *Psychonomic Bulletin & Review, 22*(3), 629–636.

Smallwood, J., Fishman, D.J., & Schooler, J.W. (2007). Counting the cost of an absent mind: Mind wandering as an underrecognized influence on educational performance. *Psychonomic Bulletin & Review, 14*(2), 230–236.

Smallwood, J., & Schooler, J.W. (2015). The science of mind wandering: Empirically navigating the stream of consciousness. *Annual Review of Psychology, 66*, 487–518.

Sood, A., & Jones, D.T. (2013). On mind wandering, attention, brain networks, and meditation. *Explore, 9*(3), 136–141.

Veraksa, A.N., Gavrilova, M.N., Bukhalenkova, D.A., Almazova, O., Veraksa, N.E., & Colliver, Y. (2019). Does Batman™ affect EF because he is benevolent or skillful? The effect of different pretend roles on pre-schoolers' executive functions. *Early Child Development and Care*, 1–10.

White, R.E., Prager, E.O., Schaefer, C., Kross, E., Duckworth, A.L., & Carlson, S.M. (2017). The "Batman Effect": Improving perseverance in young children. *Child Development, 88*(5), 1563–1571.

Zenner, C., Herrnleben-Kurz, S., & Walach, H. (2014). Mindfulness-based interventions in schools: A systematic review and meta-analysis. *Frontiers in Psychology, 5*, 603.

Zoogman, S., Goldberg, S.B., Hoyt, W.T., & Miller, L. (2015). Mindfulness interventions with youth: A meta-analysis. *Mindfulness, 6*(2), 290–302.

Thanks!

A big thanks goes to our wonderful illustrator Marcus Wilke, who equipped himself with sharpened pencils, soft brushes, and a ton of paint and watercolor paper to join us in Charlie's adventures and bring our characters to life on paper.

We also thank our dear editor, Susanne Lauri, at Hogrefe for her tireless commitment, her support with all our ideas, big and small, and the enthusiasm she has shown for our bunny world.

We were especially pleased with the large amount of valuable, helpful, and imaginative feedback from our test readers. Without you, Charlie's adventure would not be what it is today. Our thanks go to the following children, parents, and professionals:

Aidan, Eileen, and Fionn with Deborah
Alessandro and Raúl with Susana
Aline
Amélie and Elin with Gregor and Christine
Amrita with Angela
Amy, Anna, Celestina, Daniel, Layla, Matthias, Naiara, Sheila, and Zahira with Rosanna

Andreas with Denise
Anne with Maja
Annika with Evelyne
Ben with Nadine
Celine, Fiola, and Julian with Nadine
David with Daniela
David and Kevin with Melanie
Diego with Inés
Elin and Janick with Catherine
Emilie with Manuela
Emma with Birgit
Fabian and Julian with Andrea
Gabriel and Iléa with Fabian and Maya
Geli
Giuachin, Joséphine, and Ruben with Angela
Ima with Coni
Isabella and Johanna with Nadja
Jael and Janik with Nadine
Joëlle and Lars with Marion
Joelle and Simon with Denise
Juliy and Sophia
Kamy with Anjna
Kiana, Nayla, and Tim with Sarah
Laura and Lisa
Levin and Ruben with Benita
Liliane

Linda with Sabine
Livia and Matteo with Sonja
Livia and Ronja with Manuela
Lorena with Saskia
Luana and Noëmi with Chantal
Maël and Milo with Marc
Mika with Fabienne
Monika
Nils and Nina with Christine
Opfikon Elementary School's first grade class with Sarah
Paul with Beke
Sabrina with Pia
Santiago with Bettina
Selina and Chiara with Barbara
Sieglinde
Tim and Nick with Manuela and Thomas
Tim with Nicole
Veronika and Martin
Zino with Claudia
Zoé with Sandra

The Authors

Stefanie Heyden and **Fabian Grolimund** are psychologists and authors. They hope that their work will help children to be successful in school and to discover the joy of learning. They especially take pleasure in using creativity and imagination to produce anything new: good stories and practical guidebooks, as well as interesting seminars and short films for parents, teachers, children, and young people. What they enjoy most is sitting together in cafés, bouncing ideas back and forth.

The Illustrator

Marcus Wilke has been a freelance illustrator for more than 15 years. What he loves most about his job is the diversity of his clients, which include advertising agencies, private customers, and publishing houses.

For him, illustrating is both great work and great fun. He gets his creative ideas in the silence of the great outdoors and in his garden.

School
Lily pond
Ice cream parlor